"Finding Your Voice as a Beg[inning Marriage and Family Therapist is a] compelling, and utterly usabl[e book full of intentional,] transformative conversations– [...] chapters hit the right notes i[...........................], and critical consciousness. The tone is both validating and gently challenging and the personal stories of the authors and trainees, and the discussions that follow, provide rich learning for educators, supervisors, and new professionals. This book is truly like no other in the field of systemic family therapy and I hope it is read widely."

Mudita Rastogi, PhD, LMFT,
Aspire Consulting and Therapy, Arlington Heights, Illinois, USA

"What a gift to the field! Readers will be moved by the openness, vulnerability, and courage through which Stone and ChenFeng invite beginning and seasoned therapists to engage in self-of-the-therapist work that centers marginalized experience. They bring abstract concepts such as justice, equity, and critical consciousness to life, empowering new therapists and encouraging humility and accountability by those in power positions. It is the perfect addition to our curriculum and will forever change how I teach and supervise."

Carmen Knudson-Martin, PhD,
Professor and Director of Marriage, Couple, and Family Therapy, Lewis & Clark College, Portland, USA, and co-author of *Socioculturally Attuned Family Therapy: Guidelines for Equitable Theory and Practice* (Routledge)

"This book speaks to the soul of emerging couple and family therapists! *Finding Your Voice as a Beginning Marriage and Family Therapist* takes you on an intimate journey through C/MFT students' lived experiences with empowerment, invisibility, and oppression in programs. Each chapter provides reflective questions designed to engage the reader in their own personal and professional development. The book is a resource and therefore mandatory for beginning C/MFT students. It is a must read for faculty members who desire to build their consciousness, relate, supervise, and teach from inclusive frameworks. The authors deserve applause for this contemporary and transformative book."

Stephanie Brooks, PhD, LCSW, LMFT,
Associate Dean for Health Professions and Clinical Professor of Couple and Family Therapy, Drexel University, Philadelphia, USA, and Executive Consultant, American Association for Marriage and Family Therapy, Minority Fellowship Programs

"*Finding Your Voice as a Beginning Marriage and Family Therapist* is an invaluable resource to those entering the field, providing an exceptional step-by-step approach for developing the self of the therapist within one's broader sociocultural contexts. Drs. Dana J. Stone and Jessica L. ChenFeng gently invite readers to reflect on the complexity of the person they bring into the room, making it safe to explore some of the most challenging topics in supervision and training. This book belongs in every MFT's library."

Diane R. Gehart, PhD,
Professor, California State University, Northridge, USA, and author of
Mastering Competencies in Family Therapy

"*Finding Your Voice as a Beginning Marriage and Family Therapist* is bound to validate, inspire, and empower therapists from marginalized backgrounds who are engaged in challenging self-work within systems that continue to oppress them. Readers are likely to receive much-needed validation from the numerous vulnerable testimonies of Drs. Stone and ChenFeng, and their colleagues. The authors provide exercises that help transfer the validation found within these pages to processes of advancing personal growth and knitting together culturally affirming communities within the MFT profession."

Timothy Baima, PhD,
Associate Professor at Palo Alto University, USA

"The book *Finding Your Voice as a Beginning Marriage and Family Therapist* is an essential read for anyone in the field of marriage and family therapy. As stated by the co-authors, the chapters sensitively cover "self-of-the-therapist" areas including: theories and frameworks; key relational terms and frameworks; and critical systemic perspectives. The reflection questions at the end of each chapter as well as the career journeys shared throughout by Dr. Dana J. Stone and Dr. Jessica L. ChenFeng, will be quite useful for and deeply valued by all readers."

Matthew R. Mock, PhD,
Professor of Counseling Psychology, John F. Kennedy University,
Pleasant Hill, California, USA

Finding Your Voice as a Beginning Marriage and Family Therapist

Finding Your Voice as a Beginning Marriage and Family Therapist provides support to early career marriage and family therapists who seek authentic and meaningful connections with themselves, their colleagues, and the clients they serve.

The book addresses a lack of resources for early career therapists during professional formation, particularly for those who have marginalized aspects of their identity. Readers will move toward celebrating their varied social contextual selves to gain a sense of empowerment, allowing themselves to fully engage in their educational, clinical, and supervisory journey. The authors offer unique insights on the literature of clinical training as well as authentic stories from early career as well as more seasoned MFTs. There are exercises for the reader and practical skills for active engagement in their own development. Reflection questions at the end of each chapter can be used for personal reflection or to frame dialogue with classmates and colleagues.

Adaptable for use in the classroom, support groups, and in group/individual supervision settings, *Finding Your Voice as a Beginning Marriage and Family Therapist* is an essential resource for students and beginner clinicians.

Dana J. Stone, PhD, LMFT, is an Associate Professor at California State University, Northridge, USA, in the Marriage and Family Therapy Program, and an AAMFT Approved Supervisor. She identifies as Black-White Biracial and is the first person in her immediate family to achieve degrees in higher education. Her research includes deepening understanding of the biracial experience, expanding the meaning of culturally sensitive supervision, and exploring diversity in the field of MFT. She lives in Moorpark, California, with her husband and rescue pup.

Jessica L. ChenFeng, PhD, LMFT, is Associate Professor of Medical Education and Associate Director of Physician Vitality at Loma Linda University, California, USA, and an AAMFT Approved Supervisor. Her research, writing, and clinical work centers around sociocontextual issues such as gender and power, Asian American identity, and spirituality. She identifies as a second-generation Taiwanese American liberative educator and lives in Montclair, California, with her husband, their young toddler, and miniature Schnauzer.

Finding Your Voice as a Beginning Marriage and Family Therapist

DANA J. STONE AND JESSICA L. CHENFENG

Routledge
Taylor & Francis Group
NEW YORK AND LONDON

First published 2020
by Routledge
52 Vanderbilt Avenue, New York, NY 10017

and by Routledge
2 Park Square, Milton Park, Abingdon, Oxon, OX14 4RN

Routledge is an imprint of the Taylor & Francis Group, an informa business

© 2020 Taylor & Francis

The right of Dana J. Stone and Jessica L. ChenFeng to be identified as authors of this work has been asserted by them in accordance with sections 77 and 78 of the Copyright, Designs and Patents Act 1988.

All rights reserved. No part of this book may be reprinted or reproduced or utilized in any form or by any electronic, mechanical, or other means, now known or hereafter invented, including photocopying and recording, or in any information storage or retrieval system, without permission in writing from the publishers.

Trademark notice: Product or corporate names may be trademarks or registered trademarks, and are used only for identification and explanation without intent to infringe.

Library of Congress Cataloging-in-Publication Data
A catalog record for this title has been requested

ISBN: 978-1-138-29044-0 (hbk)
ISBN: 978-1-138-29045-7 (pbk)
ISBN: 978-1-315-26619-0 (ebk)

Typeset in Dante and Avenir
by Swales & Willis, Exeter, Devon, UK

For the therapist in training who is wondering if you are fit for this work,
feeling as though you don't belong
and that you might never become a good enough therapist,
this book is for you.

The paperback cover image is a photo of a quilt Dana made and that Jessica digitally reworked. It represents our shared creativity and connectedness. When our hearts are open, we can experience the colorful seasons of growth—sometimes vibrant and energizing, and other times seemingly dull, dormant, and in need of rest. All of these seasons move us toward flourishing and fullness of heart and connection.

Contents

	Acknowledgments	x
1	Introduction	1
2	Our Own Stories	20
3	Difficult and Unfulfilling Training Experiences	42
4	Meaningful and Fulfilling Training Experiences	60
5	Students' and Supervisees' Stories	77
6	Preparing and Developing the Self-of-the-Trainee	106
7	Moving Toward Sociocultural Relational Connection	138
8	Establishing a Foundation for a Career of Being Known and Knowing Others	151
	Appendix: List of Resources	172
	Index	174

Acknowledgments

We want to acknowledge the editors at Routledge who saw in us a potential to contribute something meaningful to the field. Thank you for valuing the voices of two women of color and imagining with us what this book could be. Your support, knowledge, and guidance along the way granted us courage to persist through writing our very first book.

We also want to express gratitude to the students/supervisees, colleagues, and friends who offered their stories and voices to this book. Thank you for sharing of yourselves so that future therapists could know sooner than later, that they are seen and valued.

Dana

I am so grateful to my co-author, colleague, and most importantly my friend, Jessica ChenFeng. From the first day I met you, I was inspired by your presence, your spirit, and the values you shared about the field of marriage and family therapy and regarding people in general. You have served as a support, a sounding board, a mentor, and a collaborator in the few years that we have known each other. It was in large part through my conversations with you, Jessica, that I was inspired go farther on my own journey as an MFT, educator, supervisor, and whole person. Our conversations have deepened my understanding of myself and sparked my desire to understand others even more. You have helped me grow my fire for wholeness, equity, and social justice in the way that I live and in the work that I do every day.

I am also so grateful to the students and supervisees who have allowed me to be a part of their journey to becoming an MFT. It has been such a gift and privilege to witness the growth and development and to be asked for support and guidance. My stance has always been that I am a lifelong learner and that I have more to gain from the experiences of my students and supervisees than I may have to offer them. I have also been humbled and honored when I earn their trust to walk beside them on their self-of-the-therapist journeys. It has been such a gift to teach and supervise so many amazing people, and to know that you are out there making your own way and helping others on their journeys.

I would like to acknowledge and thank some of the significant people in the education and training who "saw" me and intentionally offered guidance to me on my journey. My early career clinical supervisor, Nicole Gunderson, for caring so deeply and gently guiding me during my first year as a therapist trainee. Jan Ewing for seeing me and my potential when I was a master's student, and helping me to understand that I was a good candidate for a doctorate. Linna Wang for reading my first literature review about biracial identity and telling me it was something I should pursue researching further. Megan Dolbin-MacNab, my doctoral clinical supervisor, dissertation chair, and amazing mentor into the professoriate. I looked up to you from the moment I met you, and it was with your unwavering support through all of the years of my doctoral work that I made it to professor. Katherine Allen, who saw the teacher in me and guided me to find the heart of my career: teaching. Deanna Linville, Jeff Todahl, and John Miller for your supervision of supervision, mentorship, and guidance while I was a pre-doc and visiting instructor.

I would also like to express my gratefulness for the friendships in my life that have brought me joy, have challenged me, have helped to grow, and have supported and sustained me. I have girlfriends from childhood, two best friends, and college friends, dear friends from my masters and doctoral program, and many friends I've made on this MFT journey in addition to those friends I have made since becoming a professor, who have helped me to see myself and my potential as extraordinary. Thank you for always believing in me and cheering me on as I have pursued my dreams.

Finally, I would like to thank my family. My husband and partner in life, Christopher, for always knowing how to help me hold onto my dreams, and for always without question, supporting every crazy idea I've had so far when it comes to work and career. You are an incredible partner. Thank you to my mom for passing on the will and desire to write and of course for always believing in me, too. Thank you as well to my dad and my brothers for your part in helping me to understand myself better. I also want to thank those in my family who started paving the path before me, my grandmothers and my grandfathers, and whose legacies live on in me. It is my hope that I widen the path and expand possibilities for those who come after me.

Jessica
In writing this book, I have thought often about the clients who have given me the honor of walking alongside them. Thank you for what you have taught me in your openness to being seen. I am grateful to the amazing students who opened themselves up to discomfort and tension as we grew together, and for challenging me to see with new lenses.

There have been many amazing mentors who have supported me in finding my voice. Dr. Carmen Knudson-Martin, thank you for seeing, challenging, validating, and mentoring me these last nine years. I would not be who and where I am in feeling fulfilled in a meaningful career without your guidance and paving the way. Dr. Barbara Hernandez, thank you for your confidence in and encouraging me from my first quarter in the doctoral program until now. You instilled courage in me to open the door to writing and I am blessed to work with you and be the recipient of your affirmation and trust. To my colleagues in CSUN's Department of Educational Psychology and Counseling, thank you for seeing my potential as a new doctoral graduate. To launch my career in such a supportive and nurturing environment, to work alongside faculty committed to justice and equity, I could not have asked for more.

I have a network of remarkable people who have supported me and our family through the countless personal and professional transitions during the writing of this book. Thank you Jeney and Mark Park Hearn, Sandy and Scott Kim, Sarah Ling, Joanne Chen, Jenny Baek, Fernanda Oh, and Sophia Lee. I am grateful for the incredible MFT friends who keep me grounded and open-hearted: Justine D'Arrigo-Patrick, Lisa Esmiol, Lana Kim, Marj Castronova, Migum Gweon, and Esther Lee.

Mom and dad, you have been my champions from the beginning. Your relentless support and unwavering trust in me have given me the foundation to flourish and develop such a meaningful career. Jackie, you're my bad-ass full-time working mom *mei-mei*. You are a daily reminder to me that Asian American women are phenomenal and that I got this.

To my partner for life, Andre. So much of my ability to speak these words and grasp these ideas is because of your healing presence in my life. Thank you for modeling humility, willingness to learn, and openness to influence. The way you believe in me, push me toward excellence, and offer (sometimes without permission) critical feedback, makes me a better educator, supervisor, and clinician. To my *bao-bei* Justus: even when I am spending my days away from you because of work, it is because of you that all of this matters. As my research and writing transforms me, I hope that it helps me to shape your world and the world to come so that your generation will use your voice for good.

Dana, there is no other person with whom I could have co-authored a book such as ours. Thank you for believing in me and us even through my first full-term pregnancy and the ups and downs of Justus' first year of life. What a priceless gift to enjoy authentic sisterhood and be able to discuss theoretical frameworks, white cisheteropatriarchy, and write for hours with the same person! I have such admiration for your devotion to students and anything you commit to. You are a true gem—your authenticity, integrity, and grace always renew me. Thank you for the critical role you played in helping me find my voice when I became a new professor and for the abiding support that allowed me to flourish these last few years. I am blessed and honored to call you friend, colleague, and now co-author.

Introduction 1

It means so much to us that you have picked up this book. We have tried our best to consider who you might be and how this book can be of support to you in your growth as a marriage and family therapist. Through the planning and writing of this manuscript, we hold in our hearts the students/supervisees, professors/supervisors and colleagues who have shaped who we are and continue to strive to be. As such, we acknowledge that this is a book that could be written because of the transformative relationships and trustworthy growth processes and spaces in our own lives. While the pages ahead will have many concepts, theories, and practical guidelines, our intention is to move us toward authentic relational connections that will feed back into creating a sustainable and meaningful journey as marriage and family therapists (MFTs).

This book is possible because of the transformative relationship the two of us have shared, as well as our communities and network of relationships established over the years. Through the four years we taught and worked together, we shared countless conversations about our own training experiences—what we experienced, what we wish we knew, what we valued and what challenged us—as well as the ongoing experiences of our students/trainees and how to support them in their development. This book represents all those hours of dialogue and mentorship. It is written for our younger selves as much as it is written for the next generation of developing clinicians.

One of the privileges we share is our educational background and the access to resources and social capital this offers us. While we have absorbed much of what we have gained and the knowledge that has transformed our lives, we do not consider this book to be a "how to" manual or a way for us to share expert knowledge. It is rather, a compilation and an overflow of that which has catalyzed growth and transformation in our lives thus far. We are and will continue to be learners—being transformed as we seek to transform—for the rest of our lives. We hope to learn with and from you, so we welcome your reflections.

While the title of the book clearly indicates that this is meant for the beginning/developing therapist, we believe that it is just as beneficial for any of us—whether we are students, licensed therapists, or supervisors—if we hope for more authentic and meaningful connections with ourselves and those with whom we work. There is a particular type of audience that we are centering as our reader—those who have marginalized aspects of their identity. In our years of education and clinical training, we rarely encountered resources that centered our marginalized identities and so we hope to offer that to our readers. At the same time, we also acknowledge those with more or completely privileged identities; we look forward to this book offering you ways to expand your awareness for more authentic connection.

Engagement with the Book

We imagine that there are countless ways to best utilize this book. Certainly, it is something a reader can use on their own, but our encouragement is that this book is used in community, whether that is with friends, colleagues, classmates, or in a graduate course. We hope you will create time, space, and energy to engage with it.

This book is also meant to encourage interaction that goes beyond academic knowledge. Because we hope it will impact relationships and growth processes, it may require a different kind of presence from the reader—a presence of an *open mind*, an *open heart*, and *open hands*. This openness is also about assuming positive intention of others along the way. There will be content to challenge what you know, questions to move you to self-reflection, and ways to transform relationships. At the end of most chapters (all of Chapter 6 is a workbook for self-reflection), we offer questions for reflection for you to use for your own journaling or in dialogue with others.

This chapter highlights some of the theories and frameworks that shape our ways of engaging with this material. There is also a glossary of terms that we will use throughout the book. The rest of the book has three sections: (A) in Chapter 2, we share our own stories; (B) in Chapters 3, 4, and 5, we review the literature regarding difficult and meaningful training experiences and share the narratives of supervisees/students; (C) in Chapters 6, 7, and 8, we offer concrete ideas for self-growth, relational growth, and sustainability.

Self-of-the-Therapist

This book is about growing the self-of-the-therapist. Self or person of the therapist is centered in the idea of that the therapist, in their training and throughout their career, must be self-aware and have an ongoing commitment to developing self-awareness, to determine what aspects of the self can be utilized for or brought into therapy. Aponte's person of the therapist training model "facilitates therapists' more conscious, freer, and purposeful use of themselves" within the therapeutic context with clients (Aponte & Carlsen, 2009, p. 396). This model was developed with the goal to help therapists "develop greater capacity to personally engage with clients in ways that further therapeutic objectives *even as therapists are who they are* at the moment of contact with a client" (p. 397). This model of training is extensive and requires a deep commitment on the part of the therapist in training to engage in ongoing personal work and examination of the self. While the scope of this book is not to put trainees and early career clinicians into the in depth trainings required of the person-of-the-therapist training model, it is to introduce you to the idea that trainees must take responsibility for a meaningful examination of their personal sense of self (identity), their beliefs, bias, and values and how all of those intersect and interact with the therapy they conduct with clients. Importantly, what we can borrow from Aponte's model is the emphasis on the reality that "therapists' cultural, philosophical, and spiritual values" are "contexts for therapists' judgments and choices about how they view clients and their issues" (p. 399).

Family therapist pioneer Virginia Satir also talked about the importance of the use of the self-of-the-therapist in therapy. Specifically she was referring to the therapists who work through and continue to work through their own personal issues in order to be more emotionally available in sessions with their clients (Lum, 2002). Satir believed that when therapists were in touch with, aware of, and monitoring their self, it enabled them to become "more fully human and congruent" (p. 182). This strive for congruence, through continued personal work with difficult aspects of our lived experiences, allows therapists to remain more engaged, whole, and centered with clients. Intuition and lived experiences are important aspects of a therapist's toolbox, and Satir's concept of self-of-the-therapist highlights how important it is for therapists to accept all aspects of who they are and integrate those unique aspects of ourselves into our ability to connect more deeply and to work with clients more effectively.

In our own way, we have adapted this concept of person or self-of-the-therapist in our own work and for the purposes of this book. When we refer to the self-of-the-therapist we are referring more specifically to your multifaceted identities and how those influence your lived experiences, which in turn shapes how you think, move, believe, and feel and ultimately who you will be in therapy. As trainees and early career therapists, if we take the time to really examine our whole selves and to consider the multitude of our parts and how each of those parts influences who we are as a person and as therapists, we can then remember and be encouraged to bring our whole selves into our work with clients. With confidence we can recognize the value of our uniqueness and our differences in the therapeutic context and hopefully inspire others to do the same.

Theoretical Underpinnings

Family Systems Theory

When I (Dana) was first a student in my master's program, like all MFT students, I was introduced to the concept of systems theory—the foundational framework for the field of marriage and family therapy. While all of the philosophical underpinnings of systems theory are quite complex, I would like to highlight here, briefly, what really drew me in. First and foremost, the shift away from viewing individuals in isolation to viewing individuals within relationships—family relationships to be specific. This forever solidified for me that when working with individuals, *we cannot consider them without also considering their context* (family). This was a huge shift for me, coming from an individual psychology undergraduate program. Then the introduction of first order and second order cybernetics; the family system becoming the focus and considering the impact of the therapist as a part of or affecting the family system. Then came the idea of reciprocal causality and the notion that there was no one person to blame in the family for problems, but that *every person played a part or had a role in the both the problematic and homeostatic interaction sequences*. Then the idea of the whole of the family system being more than just the sum of its parts—the wholistic view. Adding to those ideas was the concept of subjectivity and the relativistic nature—that there was no objective truth —rather, *each family or member of the family could have their own truth or understanding of what was happening*. And finally, von Bertalanffy's (1968) concept of equifinality—*that in open systems the end state or resolution can be reached by multiple pathways or means*.

Based on these premises, we see the importance of going beyond the family system—that we cannot consider individuals without considering their larger social context. While the inequitable and oppressive systems within which we live are harmful to us all (by dividing us from one another and making it hard to have true connection; certainly the consequences of these systems impact some groups more than others), we each have a role to play—related to our social location and relational power—that can move us toward more shared equity. It is possible that we each have a different experience of these dynamics, even if our social locations appear the same— it is not a framework of who is right or wrong, but rather having the same vision and hope and moving together in that direction.

Socio-Emotional Relationship Therapy

When I was a doctoral student (Jessica), I had the opportunity to be part of an ongoing research group that studied couples therapy processes focusing on gender and power. This research group was applying Socio-Emotional Relationship Therapy (SERT), founded by Carmen Knudson-Martin and Douglas Huenergardt, to clinical work with couples. Though the theory began with looking at couples and their gendered power dynamics, our conversations and research studies expanded to other contextual processes and shaped our consciousness about how to be therapists. The five principles that guide the practice of SERT continue to frame my way of understanding relationships, both personally and professionally. These are the principles (Knudson-Martin & Huenergardt, 2015).

Context Structures Personal Identities and Relational Processes

SERT situates relational issues in the larger context and not simply in the individual, the relationship or the family. We must therefore understand the social context and discourses that shape us and our clients' experiences/identities. This principle explains how we understand not only our clients but also ourselves and those with whom we are in relationship. Context always matters.

Emotion Is Contextual

Emotions are connected to the social context in which our identities are shaped. The meaning we make of ourselves and experiences is constructed in context and the emotions we feel and express are an outflow of that process. As we seek to understand ourselves and others, we explore the connection between what we and others feel as part of our contextual identities.

Power Is Relational

Relational power is about influence in the relationship. Whose preferences, perspectives, or reality are attended to/privileged? This is present in any relationship dynamic and worth reflecting upon even in professional relationships. We hope that the resources in this book will support you to better identify and respond to the relational power in your life.

Relationships Should Mutually Support Each Partner

This SERT principle establishes that there should be mutual support in couples' relationships. Expanding this beyond the couple dynamic, when we seek authenticity in our relational connections, we are hoping for a reciprocity and mutuality that allows us to feel seen by and to see the other.

Therapists Must Actively Intervene in Social Processes

Without examining how we, as therapists, absorb societal discourses, we too can perpetuate inequitable dynamics not only with clients but in our own lives/relationships. SERT takes the stance that we are active interveners in social processes. We too believe that whether we are in the role of the therapist or in our own professional and personal relationships, we must posture ourselves to be actively engaged in addressing societal disparities and contributing to the development of equity.

Risks and Benefits of This Journey

We see this book as an invitation to a lifelong journey of personal growth and self-discovery that can inspire you to deepen relationships with colleagues, supervisors, and clients. Work on the *self*, and bringing your whole self into the work and working relationships you have in your life is risky. What we mean by this is that there is always the chance that you may be hurt or that you may even hurt others on the journey. To be whole means to be authentic and to share your emotional parts with others. When people choose to engage with their whole *self*, there is a level of vulnerability because of the uncertainty of how others may react or respond to your effort. Dr. Brené Brown, sharing her years of research, talked about vulnerability on a public stage in her 2010 TEDTalk, *The Power of Vulnerability*. She said that to build connecting relationships with others, we must have courage to "tell the story of who [we] are with a whole heart," which also requires authenticity "to let go of who [we] think [we] should be in order to be who [we actually] are." When we allow ourselves to be vulnerable in relationship with others, we are making an investment that "may or may not work out." While self-care is a huge topic on its own and we could devote another book to this, we want to emphasize that this process of moving toward vulnerability and authenticity calls for much kindness to self and others. It requires tending to ourselves as physical, relational, intellectual, spiritual beings. Because we believe in the long-lasting benefit of whole hearted and authentic engagement of your sociocultural self on your journey to becoming an MFT, we offer some suggestions for how to take care of yourself along the way.

- Caring for our physical selves
    - Visiting our health care provider of choice for check-ups (acupuncturist, naturopath, physician, osteopath, cultural healer, etc.)
    - Keeping our bodies engaged in physical activities and movement that are life-giving
    - Getting adequate nutrition through whole foods, not forgetting wisdom from own cultural traditions
    - Spending time in natural, non-technological environments

- Caring for our social/relational selves
    - Connecting with friends we feel seen by—scheduling regular meal or coffee dates

- Scheduling time to be or chat with family/family of choice
- Scheduling couples or family therapy to support relational dynamics

• Caring for our intellectual selves

- Creating time to invest in non-academic interests/hobbies—joining a book club, visiting the museum, taking a cooking/art class, listening to a new podcast

• Caring for our spiritual selves

- Taking time to be in nature—visiting a local park/garden, driving to the beach/mountains, or scheduling a vacation to be in the natural environment
- Investing in your religious/spiritual community—starting practices or joining groups
- Engaging in mindfulness or meditation practices

Glossary of Terms

The purpose of the glossary at the start of this book is to introduce important terms and concepts that have informed our own growth, thinking, and the why for bringing our whole selves into our work as MFTs. This glossary of terms is by no means exhaustive, but should help as you dive deeper into your reading of the text. We understand that some readers will be familiar with these terms because of your educational or social context. For others, we see this book as an introduction to such concepts and encourage you to pursue knowledge and awareness beyond this text. We have placed the glossary of terms at the beginning, as a sort of guiding framework, that will be easy to flip back to from time to time as you read other parts of the book. Another note about the glossary is that we have put the terms in alphabetical order, which should help when you are using it as a reference.

Colonialism

The West has a long history of colonizing peoples and territories. "Settler colonialism is a persistent social and political formation in which newcomers/colonizers/settlers come to a place, claim it as their own, and do whatever it takes to disappear the indigenous peoples that are there" (Arvin, Tuck, & Morrill, 2013, p. 12). In the process of colonizing, colonizers privilege the social, cultural, and symbolic capital of colonizers and marginalize indigenous ways of life (McDowell & Hernandez, 2010 as cited in McDowell, 2015, p. 3). This way of being and thinking permeates our consciousness and it influences our lives and shapes the practices in all fields. In our MFT field, it shows up in the use of evidence-based practices without consideration of their cross-cultural relevance or the privileging of westernized theories and models of therapy for understanding and working with diverse populations in the United States and abroad (McDowell, 2015).

Contextual Consciousness

We think of contextual consciousness as the clinical application of critical consciousness in the therapy space. Esmiol, Knudson-Martin, and Delgado (2012) define it as having three dimensions:

> (a) consciousness about the inherent power differentials in a person's social contexts, including gender, race, socioeconomic status, and sexual orientation; (b) sensitivity to clients' unique experiences within these different contexts; and (c) attention to the intersection of the larger context with clients' relational processes and presenting issues.
> (p. 574)

Contextual Differentiation

This concept arose from my (Jessica) clinical work with Asian American populations (ChenFeng, 2018). It is how I characterize much of what I was supporting clients toward—being contextually differentiated.

> If individual differentiation is the ability to identify one's own thoughts and feelings separately from that of the family, then contextual differentiation is identifying one's own thoughts and feelings as they are influenced by, related to, or different from one's context.
> (p. 17)

In certain contexts or with certain people, we might find ourselves being reactive in one way or another (feeling on edge, incompetent, silenced, etc.). It is possible that we, in all the aspects of our social location, are reacting to something in our context that further marginalizes our sense of self as it relates to other people's social location or the context's dominant culture. Rather than internalizing those exchanges as something inferior about us, increasing contextual differentiation allows us to be informed about who we are as contextual selves interacting in contextual spaces/relationships. This awareness then increases our ability to choose how we want to respond instead of react.

Critical Consciousness

The literature offers many ways of conceptualizing critical consciousness, which emerges from the process of *conscientization*, or consciousness-raising (Freire, 2000). Critical consciousness is "the ability to recognize and challenge oppressive and dehumanizing political, economic, and social systems" (Garcia et al., 2009, p. 20). Recognizing these systems requires gaining knowledge and awareness (of self, other, and structures) and challenging the systems, however this might look for each person. Some of us challenge oppressive systems at the individual relational level and others choose to engage sociopolitically with collective action. We see critical consciousness as something each of us is continually working to raise in our own lives; we do not ever fully arrive at a state of having complete critical consciousness.

Cultural Humility

The concept of humility has both interpersonal and intrapersonal dimensions (Davis et al., 2011). Humble individuals are other-oriented instead of self-focused (interpersonal), demonstrated through their respect of others and their lack of superiority. They also have an accurate view of themselves (intrapersonal). Thus the concept of cultural humility "involves the ability to maintain an interpersonal stance that is other-oriented (or open to the other) in relation to aspects of cultural identity that are most important to the client" (Hook et al., 2013, p. 354). While it is important to develop specific skills, we appreciate the focus of cultural humility as being a virtue or disposition. When we are culturally humble, we still strive to be knowledgeable and informed, while also maintaining awareness that we are limited in our understanding of clients' cultural realities. This hopefully compels us to continue to maintain a curious and humble stance.

Culture

Hays (2008) defines culture broadly, as a term that encompasses people of ethnic and non-ethnic groups with "traditions of thought and behavior such as language and history that can be socially acquired, shared, and passed on to new generations" (p. 14). According to Thomas and Schwarzbaum (2017), culture organizes people's lives and how they view themselves which is a major influence and determinant for individual identity development. It is also referred to as "collective meaning-making, shared knowledge and attitudes, and conceptual frameworks for understanding the universe …" (McDowell et al., 2017, p. 14). Many factors contribute to culture such as customs, traditions, celebrations, rituals, heritage, history, legacies, etc., and each aspect is affected by power, privilege, and bias.

Diversity and Equity

We want to clarify the use of these two terms because they are often confused with one another. "Diversity attends to issues of inclusion and focuses on WHO is included" (Hardy, 2016, p. 7). For example, we could say "There is much racial diversity in my supervision group" and that would mean that there is representation of different racial backgrounds in the people who make up this group. Equity is about the "equitable distribution of power" (Hardy, 2016, p. 7). To work toward equity is to care about justice, so it is possible for a supervision group, for example, to have racial diversity, but not necessarily equity. Equity would mean that each person in the group has a felt sense of voice, access, and importance in that shared space. Representation/diversity matters, but equity is the larger picture goal.

Dominant Discourses

Discourses are a framework for understanding the sociocultural and historical contexts within which people live (Freedman & Combs, 1996). They are socially constructed structures that shape how we think about ourselves and others, as well as how we relate to and interact with others. Dominant discourses are influenced by the power structures in society and they shape norms and expectations for cultures which are often oppressive. Dominant discourses about race, gender, and sexual orientation for example can foster structural inequities due to racist, sexist, and heteronormative ideologies. When such ideologies prevail, they may become internalized by the individual, family, or community, and shape the narratives or stories they tell themselves (and others) about what it means to be a Black, Queer, woman for example. Those discourses significantly affect how that person experiences the world around them, how they behave, and how they evaluate their own life (Gehart, 2018).

Ethnicity

Ethnicity is influenced by a person's race, but is not limited to race. Ethnicity is often thought of as the synthesis of biology, ancestry, and cultural factors that culminate in shared values and customs that are transmitted across generations (McGoldrick et al., 2005). Ethnicity may refer to nationality and country of origin or it can refer to a religion or lifestyle (Robinson-Wood, 2017). In the United States, ethnic groups are often categorized broadly, using terms like Asian to account for all groups such as Japanese and Chinese which each have numerous subgroups within them. According to Phinney (1996), ethnicity is "conceptualized as a discrete categorical variable" (as cited in Hays, 2008, p. 13) but is actually variable based on historical context, physical location, situation, and developmental phase of the individual or group.

Intersectionality

A term coined in 1989, when Kimberlé Crenshaw was referring to the marginalization of Black women, and the impossibility of discussing the issues without considering *both* gender *and* race, rather than focusing on gender *or* race (Crenshaw, 1989). In other words the marginalization of Black women occurs at the intersection of race and gender. Over the years the theory of intersectionality has evolved to and been utilized across disciplines and meanings have been adapted. For the purpose of our book, intersectionality refers to the interconnectedness of race, gender, and other aspects of the socially constructed categories of our identities (our social location) and how they intersect, interrelate, and interact with systems of oppression, power, and privilege to shape our experiences (Coates, Ferber, & Brunsma, 2018; Sorrells, 2016).

Oppression

Oppression reflects the sociocultural and sociopolitical values of a society (Thomas & Schwarzbaum, 2017). It represents the ways in which people or groups of people with particular socially constructed identity statuses are overlooked, undervalued, dismissed, or mistreated. Oppression by its very nature is relational, as it is the relationships between the dominant and nondominant groups that oppressive acts or forces are perpetuated. Oppression can occur at the personal, interpersonal, and social level (Thomas & Schwarzbaum, 2017). Oppressive forces deny equal access and equal rights to subordinated social groups. Oppression stigmatizes and disempowers visible and invisible identities (Robinson-Wood, 2017). Bias plus power equals the *isms*. Some of the more commonly known *isms* or forms of oppression operating in American society include: ableism, ageism, anti-semitism, audism, classism, colonialism, colorism, ethnocentrism, heterosexism, racism, sexism, sizeism, and xenophobia. "The task of resisting our own oppression does not relieve us of the responsibility of acknowledging our complicity in the oppression of others" (Tatum, 1997, p. 39).

Power

Power is a complex concept, difficult to define, even with its mention in many diversity and family therapy texts and articles. Though power manifests itself in institutions, structures, and systems, at the foundation it is always relational as it plays out in every relationship. A person with power can impose their will or values on another person or group of people (McDowell, 2015). Further, the relational and bidirectional views offer that

> power is not held as a possession or intrinsic to an individual. It depends on, or resides in, the relationship between people fueled by the nature of the relationship and the resources each has to potentially bring to bear on the other.
>
> (McDowell, 2015, p. 6)

McDowell further expands the definition of power to include Foucault's perspective of power as multidirectional. In other words, power is enacted and "discursive, embedded in the creation of knowledge, and our understanding of what is true. Knowledge is power and the powerful have greater influences on what is defined as truth and reality" (p. 6) which ultimately organizes our societies and shapes our lives. Power is often unequally distributed and typically lies in the hands of colonizers, who make decisions that benefit their own group and control access to resources, which contributes to and perpetuates structural inequality and oppression of the "other." In discussing significant relationships, Knudson-Martin (2013) highlights how those with power are "less responsive to their partners' feelings and interests; the less powerful have difficulty influencing them and their needs and interests are less likely to be supported in the relationship" (p. 15). This translates to other types of relationships where those with power are less aware of the needs and experiences of those with less power while the latter tend to be very aware of the norms and expectations of the person/group with more power.

Privilege

Peggy McIntosh (2008) explained the concept of privilege in her essay "Unpacking the Invisible Knapsack" as unearned and often unacknowledged advantages given to dominant social groups. It is often conceived of as normative and as a right. Dominant social groups (Whites, males, heterosexuals) benefit at the expense of non-dominant groups (African Americans, females, LGBTQIA). Privilege has effects on both groups of people, and leads to "systems of oppression based on dominance and subordination" (Hernandez-Wolfe & McDowell, 2012, p. 164). In simple terms, privilege refers to unearned civil rights, societal benefits, and advantages granted based solely on a particular identity status (e.g. White privilege, male privilege, heterosexual privilege) (McGeorge & Carlson, 2011). In order to dismantle privilege, we must first acknowledge our own unearned privilege(s) and then we must take steps to deconstruct systems of advantage (McIntosh, 2008).

Race

Race is a socially constructed concept created to classify people based primarily on physical characteristics such as skin color, hair texture, and facial features (Spickard, 1992). What we know about racial categories is that there is often greater variability within racial groups than between them. Race is not rooted in biology, rather it is rooted in the economic and social climate of slavery in the United States (Tatum, 1997). Although race is a social construction, because it has become a part of our identity, race matters personally and socially for many people and has significant implications in American society (Hays, 2008; Tatum, 1997). Racial categories place people and groups into minority–majority or marginalized–dominant groupings. These groupings, like much of what we discuss, are affected by the notions of power, privilege, and oppression.

Social Justice

"Social justice is about issues of equity, especially the equitable distribution of power. When social justice is the focal point, it places the issues of power, powerlessness, privilege, and subjugation under careful scrutiny" (Hardy & Bobes, 2016, p. 7). As therapists who operate within a framework of critically informed clinical practice, activism and social action are an integral part of the therapeutic process in which clients' problems are understood as under the influences of larger sociocultural contexts (D'Arrigo-Patrick et al., 2016). This means that therapists operating from a social justice orientation raise client awareness about the connection between their presenting problems and social issues as well as work with clients to dismantle the oppressive societal structures that clients have assumed or internalized, often unconsciously, that perpetuate and maintain powerlessness and inequity (Almeida, Dolan Del-Vecchio, & Parker, 2008; D'Arrigo-Patrick et al., 2016). We are operating from the position that when therapists are social justice oriented in their clinical work, they believe that everyone deserves equal access and opportunities and so they consider the impact of social issues on their clients' presenting problems and ask questions about the effects of social issues in their clients' lives and integrate advocacy and empowerment into the goals of therapy (D'Arrigo-Patrick et al., 2016; Robinson-Wood, 2017).

Social Location and Context

Mock (2008) explains the term social location as the social and historical groups that people belong to in society that help define who we are and how we are treated. It is grounded in the myriad aspects of our identity including, but not limited to, race and ethnicity, gender, sexual orientation, religion, regionality, ability, social class or socioeconomic status (SES), and age or generation. Other authors, such as Zimmerman et al. (2016) and Burnham et al. (2008), discuss the concept of social location to acknowledge that these aspects of a person's identity help to make up the whole of a person and therefore must be considered as therapists, supervisors, and teachers. Context involves the varying realities, perspectives, and experiences we each incorporate from our own embeddedness within the various milieus of our lives (Hardy & Bobes, 2016). The contextual variables include, but are not limited to, family and culture, and more broadly local and dominant discourses that shape and frame our lived experiences. Hardy and Bobes list the following contextual variables as "critical domains of interest": ethnicity, class, gender, race, religion, sexual orientation, nationality, age, ability, and regionality (p. 6).

Summary

In this first chapter, we wanted to introduce you to our vision for this book. Because we did not have such a resource nor did the students/supervisees with whom we worked, we have written it so that those with any sort of marginalized identity(ies) feel supported and encouraged. Family systems theory and socio-emotional relationship therapy (SERT) are two of the theoretical frameworks that inform the lens through which we build our ideas. We also encourage our readers to maintain a posture of openness to the process of learning, self-growth, and possibility of authentic relational connection.

Questions for Reflection

1. What do you hope to gain from reading this book?
2. What goals do you hope to accomplish related to deepening your understanding of your social location? To raise your critical consciousness?
3. What terms were new to you? How will you expand your learning regarding those concepts?
4. Who are the peers in your life with whom you have an authentic connection and hope to share this journey of finding your

voice and flourishing as an MFT? What steps will you take to build authentic, wholehearted relationships on your academic and career journey as an MFT?

References

Almeida, R., Dolan Del-Vecchio, K., & Parker, L. (2008). *Transformative family therapy: Just families in a just society*. New York: Pearson.

Aponte, H. J., & Carlsen, J. C. (2009). An instrument for person-of-the-therapist supervision. *Journal of Marital and Family Therapy, 35*(4), 395–405.

Arvin, M., Tuck, E., & Morrill, A. (2013). Decolonizing feminism: Challenging connections between settler colonialism and heteropatriarchy. *Feminist Formations, 25*(1), 8–34.

Burnham, J., Palma, D. A., Whitehouse, L. (2008). Learning as a context for differences and differences as a context for learning. *Journal of Family Therapy, 30*, 529–542

ChenFeng, J. (2018).Integration of self and family: Asian American Christians in the midst of white Evangelicalism and being the model minority. In E. E. Wilson & L. Nice (Eds.) *Socially just religious and spiritual interventions: Ethical uses of therapeutic power*. New York: Springer.

Coates, R. D., Ferber, A. L., & Brunsma, D. L. (2018). *The matrix of race: Social construction, intersectionality, and inequality*. Thousand Oaks, CA: Sage.

Crenshaw, K. (1989). Demarginalizing the intersection of race and sex: A black feminist critique of antidiscrimination doctrine. *University of Chicago Legal Forum, 1989*, 139–168.

D'Arrigo-Patrick, J., Hoff, C., Knudson-Martin, C., & Tuttle, A. (2016). Navigating critical theory and postmodernism: Social justice and therapist power in family therapy. *Family Process, 56*(3), 574–588.

Davis, D. E., Hook, J. N., Worthington, E. L., Jr., Van Tongeren, D. R., Gartner, A. L., Jennings, D. J., II., & Emmons, R. A. (2011). Relational humility: Conceptualizing and measuring humility as a personality judgment. *Journal of Personality Assessment, 93*, 225–234. doi:10.1080/00223891.2011.558871.

Esmiol, E., Knudson-Martin, C., & Delgado, S. (2012). How MFT students develop a critical contextual consciousness: A participatory action research project. *Journal of Marital and Family Therapy, 38*, 573–588.

Freedman, J., & Combs, G. (1996). *Narrative therapy: The social construction of preferred realities*. New York: Norton.

Freire, P. (2000). *Pedagogy of the oppressed*. New York: Continuum.

Garcia, M., Kosutic, I., McDowell, T., & Anderson, S. A. (2009). Raising critical consciousness in family therapy supervision. *Journal of Feminist Family Therapy, 21*, 18–38. doi:10.1080/08952830802683673.

Gehart, D. (2018). *Mastering competencies in family therapy: A practical approach to theories and clinical case documentation*. Boston, MA: Cengage.

Hardy, K. (2016). Toward the development of a multicultural relational perspective in training and supervision. In K. Hardy & T. Bobes (Eds.), *Culturally sensitive supervision and training: Diverse perspectives and practical applications* (pp. 3–10). New York: Routledge.

Hardy, K. V., & Bobes, T. (Eds.) (2016). *Culturally sensitive supervision and training: Diverse perspectives and practical applications*. New York: Routledge.

Hays, P. (2008). *Addressing cultural competencies in practice: Assessment, diagnosis and therapy* (2nd ed.). Washington, DC: American Psychological Association.

Hernandez-Wolfe, P., & McDowell, T. (2012). Speaking of privilege: Family therapy educators' journeys toward awareness and compassionate action. *Family Process, 51*, 163–178.

Hook, J., Davis, D., Owen, J., Worthington, E., & Utsey, S. (2013). Cultural humility: Measuring openness to culturally diverse clients. *Journal of Counseling Psychology, 60*(3), 353–366. doi: 10.1037/a0032595.

Knudson-Martin, C. (2013). Why power matters: Creating a foundation of mutual support in couple relationships. *Family Process, 52*(1), 5–18. doi: 10.1111/famp.12011

Knudson-Martin, C., & Huenergardt, D. (2015). Bridging emotion, societal discourse, and couple interaction in clinical practice. In C. Knudson-Martin, M. A. Wells, & S. K. Samman (Eds.), *Socio-Emotional relationship therapy: Bridging emotion, societal context, and couple interaction* (pp. 1–13). American Family Therapy Academy, Springer.

Lum, W. (2002). The use of self of the therapist. *Contemporary Family Therapy, 24*(1), 181–197.

McDowell, T. (2015). *Applying critical social theories to family therapy practice*. New York: American Family Therapy Academy, Springer.

McDowell, T., Knudson-Martin, C., & Bermudez, J. M. (2017). *Socioculturally attuned family therapy: Guidelines for equitable theory and practice*. New York: Routledge.

McGeorge, C., & Carlson, T. S. (2011). Deconstructing heterosexism: Becoming an LGB affirmative heterosexual couple and family therapist. *Journal of Marital and Family Therapy, 37*(1), 14–26.

McGoldrick, M., Pearce, J., & Giordano, J. (Eds.) (2005). *Ethnicity and family therapy* (3rd ed.). New York: Guilford.

McIntosh, P. (2008). White privilege and male privilege: A personal account of coming to see correspondences through work in women's studies. In M. McGoldrick & K. V. Hardy (Eds.), *Re-visioning family therapy: Race, cultures, and gender in clinical practice* (pp. 239–249). New York: Guilford.

Mock, M. R. (2008). Revisioning social justice: Narratives of diversity, social location and personal compassion. In M. McGoldrick & K. V. Hardy (Eds.), *Re-visioning family therapy: Race, culture, and gender in clinical practice* (2nd ed.) (pp. 425–441). New York: Guilford.

Phinney, J. S. (1996).When we talk about American ethnic groups, what do we mean? *American Psychologist, 51*, 918–927.

Robinson-Wood, T. (2017). *The convergence of race, ethnicity, and gender: Multiple identities in counseling* (5th ed.). Thousand Oaks, CA: Sage.

Sorrells, K. (2016). *Intercultural communication: Globalization and social justice* (2ed.). Thousand Oaks: Sage.

Spickard, P. R. (1992). The illogic of American racial categories. In M. P. P. Root (Ed.), *Racially mixed people in America* (pp. 12–23). Newbury Park, CA: Sage.

Tatum, B. D. (1997). *"Why are all the black kids sitting together in the cafeteria?" and other conversations about race*. New York: Basic Books.

TEDxHouston (Producer). (2010). *The power of vulnerability*: Brené Brown. Available from www.ted.com/talks/brene_brown_on_vulnerability.

Thomas, A. J., & Schwarzbaum, S. E. (2017). *Culture and identity: Life stories for counselors and therapists* (3rd ed.). Thousand Oaks, CA: Sage.

von Bertalanffy, L. (1968). *General system theory: Foundations, development, applications*. New York: George Braziller.

Zimmerman, T., Castronova, M., & ChenFeng, J. (2016). Diversity and social justice in supervision. In K. Jordan (Ed.), *Couple, marriage, and family therapy supervision*. New York: Springer.

Our Own Stories 2

We believe that who we are is everything we have in terms of how we can best serve our clients. Knowing ourselves and engaging in self-of-the-therapist growth is foundational to how we exist in the world as professors, supervisors, colleagues, and therapists. That is why we want to begin by telling you our stories. In this chapter, we reflect on our experiences of when we first began as students in the MFT field.

In the 22 years (collectively) that we have been MFT educators, we have come to see that the way that education in general, but specifically MFT education, is set up is not accessible equally nor is it relevant to all students. Much of MFT education is about the teaching of MFT theories (which we love and appreciate) and any adaptation to a particular population (racial group, religious group, etc.) is exactly that—take this theory and how can it be adapted for X population. While there has been much benefit to clients over the years with this type of method, we want to humbly suggest that it is time to revisit this process.

When a student of color learns about Bowen Family Systems Theory, resonates with it (like I did! Jessica) and wants to adapt it to a particular population (Chinese Americans, for example), what gets internalized for the student is this: "This original MFT theory, founded by a White westernized man is the right/true model and let me try to see how I can make it fit to work with my people/population of interest." This process makes it difficult for the student to consider their own culture or group's inherent strengths, interests, values, ethnic processes, paths of healing that already exist apart from the MFT theory. In the MFT education process, the student is unknowingly internalizing -isms through the education process.

We recognize that as we seek to center marginalized voices, our own first, we will do this imperfectly because of the colonization of our own education and minds. Here are our own stories, starting with our early training experiences.

Early Training Experience (Jessica)

I identify as a second-generation Taiwanese American, heterosexual, cisgender, hearing, educated, currently able-bodied, U.S. citizen, female (pronouns she/her/hers), Christian. I am married to my 1.5 generation Taiwanese American husband, who after 12 years as an urban public educator of middle school math, is now working on finishing his PhD in Education. We try our best to build a mutually supportive relationship, and parent our young toddler with delight and humility. In the last year, I have been wrestling with what it means to be a full-time working academic mom and integrating this into my sense of self.

Call into the Field

Entering the field of marriage and family therapy usually goes hand-in-hand with a call of some sort. My call came toward the end of my undergraduate studies when I was not finding fulfillment in working as a graphic designer, while at the same time perplexed and troubled by the needs of my Taiwanese American Christian church community. I was mentoring a number of younger women and was pained by what I understood at the time to be depression, anxiety, family struggles and marital discord. Little did I know that I too had a lot of baggage to sort through, but what I knew was that I wanted to help. So I took some prerequisites and applied to Fuller Theological Seminary, and that was the beginning of my journey with the field of marriage and family therapy.

Sense of Self and Others

I was in my early twenties when I began the MFT program. Much of my academic and social experience up until that point was in a context with majority Asian American classmates and peers, specifically from a conservative Asian American Christian context. But this was largely unexamined and I took for granted the Asian American cultural nuances, the heteronormative interactions, and a world that did not consciously see or discuss issues of race or cultural identity. There was a comfort, safety, and ease, but I did not have words for this—it was just my "normal."

I can look back with these reflections now, but they were not in my awareness. I was the elder of two daughters, always "good," most likely to ease the stress of my parents' marital distress. I was good at school and my friends were the popular and smart kids. I never thought about how most of my high school teachers and college professors were White, but I was used to seeing Asian American students work hard and please (impress) the teachers. They were wonderful kind teachers who wanted the best for us, but knowing how to work hard and be socially adept to please my White teachers was my internalized reality. What I knew about myself was that I could work hard, study well, achieve, engage socially—and it kept me going.

One important piece of my identity to highlight is my socialization within a largely evangelical world. Though my context was Asian American, White evangelical heteropatriarchy influenced how I internalized my sense of self and others. Intentionally or not, my Christian context was one that

> [promoted] a culture-free and color-blind church, a position on race shared with white evangelicalism … What emerges is the self-reinforcement of the Christian model minority: the maintenance of white privilege, affirmation of middle-class standing, preservation of ethnic hierarchy in American evangelicalism, and compliance in the racialized formation of Asian Americans.
>
> (Yu, 2016, pp. 3–4)

I loved the celebrations of Taiwanese culture through food, language, and holiday events, yet the theology we took for granted was devoid of cultural or historical integration of our community's context and place in American society. The truth is that I don't think any of the pastors or church leaders, myself included, were ever given the opportunity to develop critical consciousness. The insularity of the community made it so that we were able to stay comfortable within the familiar and did not have to encounter much difference. The structure of American evangelicalism was such that the primary resources we had access to were teachings by White male pastors. The intersection of my ethnic/racial identity with evangelical heritage made it too easy for me to live under the pressure of fulfilling the model minority stereotype.

Training Experience

When I began the master's program, it was the first time I was interacting regularly and closely with classmates of diverse racial backgrounds, especially White classmates. This came into my awareness because of the unease and low-grade anxiety I felt in group contexts. In group supervision settings, I found myself not knowing how to interject or speak up. The flow of conversation—people speaking up as they pleased and interjecting—was foreign to me. I felt that if I engaged in this way, it would be rude or disrespectful. I could tell that this was not the case for my peers, but regardless it left me struggling to speak my thoughts and be visible.

My supervisor during traineeship was a White heterosexual male who trained and challenged us in applying Bowenian and object relations theory to clinical practice. I have positive memories of my year at that training site, but there are specific experiences I had that gripped me with anxiety. I was seeing a mixed-race couple (older White man and a Latina woman) and the husband was addicted to pornography of Asian women. I do not remember much except for feeling the wife's anger toward me, feeling overwhelmed with stress and anxiety before and after sessions with them, feeling unsafe and nauseated, and having no idea how to work with this couple. In individual supervision, I do not recall talking about my racial and cultural identity (among many other parts of me that were struggling) and how I was personally affected by clinical work with this couple. There were clear power dynamics related to social location in this complex clinical situation that were simply not a part of supervision.

I was also a co-facilitator for a weekly Saturday parenting/child abuse support group. Every Friday night, I felt such significant anxiety that I did not rest well. In retrospect, I know that much of my anxiety had to do with feeling, appearing, and being younger, and not having my own children. It also had to do with my racial identity—my co-facilitator was an older more clinically experienced Asian woman (different from me being Asian American) and in our dynamics, I felt that I had to please her and show that I was competent. We never talked about our racial identities as being the only Asian-identified people in the large-sized parenting group. These were never brought up in supervision because it would mean that I was not competent and becoming a good family therapist. Suffice it to say, that year I "pushed through" my anxiety alone, and convinced my supervisor and myself that I was good at being a therapist and graduated.

Academic Context

One of the greatest gifts of my master's academic context was the modeling of cultural and spiritual humility by faculty and peers. I remember one evening, sitting in an Old Testament class taught by a renowned Old Testament emeritus faculty. A student asked a question about the biblical text and I remember waiting for the professor to give a clear definitive answer when he kindly said (my memory of what he said) "I don't know. The more I study the text, the less I can speak with certainty." I was impacted by the professor's gracious humility and was drawn to this refreshing experience of openness and open-handedness to life and intellectual/spiritual growth.

There was much that this professor did know, as well as many of the other faculty during my master's program, yet at the same time, they did not model knowing with being right or that others were wrong. Having grown up with an image of teachers and professors as my superiors and role models that I respected, these interactions gave me a different template for understanding relational power, a power with the other, and not a power over or under. Though I did not have language to describe my experience then, what I internalized was relating with theological authority that did not feel bigoted, narrow-minded, or condescending of others.

Reflections

You might be able to guess that I had very little critical consciousness throughout this season of my life (I was dysconscious [King, 1991]). Even though my context up until graduate school centered around ethnic, gender, and religious experiences (Asian American Christians with defined gender roles/identities), it was part of the air we all breathed. There was little reflection about these identities. While I deeply valued my master's training experience, not much changed in terms of my level of critical consciousness, except that my feeling different started to rise to the surface. Looking back, I understand the anxiety I felt to be related the Asian American model minority pressure to achieve and maintain a level of competence to my mostly White context/supervisors/professors. What I want to emphasize again is that I had no awareness of this happening, little contextual differentiation. I was merely reacting to my social context, not understanding or knowing why and the consequence was, at times, a debilitating anxiety. That is why working with ourselves (and eventually our clients) to increase critical consciousness and contextual differentiation is of utmost importance.

Early Development and Training Experiences (Dana)

I identify as a Black-White Biracial, heterosexual, cisgender female (pronouns she/her/hers), hearing, able-bodied, U.S. citizen. I am first-generation college and graduate educated. I am a person of color with awareness of my privilege due to my light skin and appearance, often mistaken for white. My racial identity is a critical and significant component of who I am. Throughout my life I experienced stigmatization from Black peers and did not feel accepted because I was a "wanna be White girl" or "not Black enough." I actually never wanted to be either Black or White, but wanted to be accepted for who I was, which was both Black *and* White. I believe racial identity, like all aspects of identity, continues to evolve and change over the life course. My Biracial identity development is centered in my life narrative and especially in my journey into the field of MFT.

Journey into the Field

Undergrad

I graduated from college with a bachelor's degree in Psychology. When I entered college I thought I wanted to be a high school English teacher, so I started out majoring in English. I loved it. But then I took my first psychology class and fell hard. I became overjoyed learning about development, cognition, behavior, and morality for example. Yet, the focus on the individual and learning about animal behavior, while fascinating, was not fueling my soul. At the time I honestly had no idea where a degree in psychology would or could take me, so I worked hard for my degree but remained unsure about my future. Unfortunately, while I was a young and impressionable undergrad, one psychology professor expressed his belief I would not make it into a doctoral program, which I understood as a requirement for a future in psychology. His words crushed me. As a first-generation college student (which did not have a name or accompanying support when I was in college) I had no idea about internships and applying for jobs or what to do upon graduation. So, when I graduated (a huge accomplishment for me personally and also for my family), I felt discouraged and unsure about where to turn. Many of my childhood friends graduated from college with degrees that would take them directly into their careers such as teaching and nursing. Several of my friends from college started graduate school or had plans to travel or join teaching corps or Peace Corps. For two years post-graduation, before I even learned what a marriage and family therapist was, I worked in retail and took courses at the local community college while trying to find my way. Eventually, I met with a college counselor there who actually told me about graduate school and the field of marriage and family therapy ... and finally something clicked!

Grad School

When I started graduate school in MFT I did not have a frame of reference for what it meant to be a master's level student and I was not quite sure what to expect from a professional training program. But during those first few classes, I knew I had found my way into something that felt so right! I loved everything about what I was learning and so many of my life experiences started making sense within the systemic and family therapy frameworks I was learning about. While I was in love with what I was learning, I admit I was still a bit lost, not quite sure how to navigate it all as a first-generation graduate student. I had chosen a private school, not really understanding all of what my options were for the degree when I applied and so began accruing student loan debt from day one. During the course of my program I faced other challenges, such as not knowing how to write an APA paper, what it would actually mean to apply for field site placements, and whether or not I should continue to work once I started seeing clients. And the messages from that single professor in undergrad haunted me ... which meant I found myself struggling with the question of whether I truly belonged.

Sense of Self

Beginning graduate school as a woman in my mid-twenties, I believed I had established a sense of security in my identity as both a female and racially: mixed race/Biracial Black-White. However, I had not considered how my overall sense of self would evolve so much more as I navigated the world of graduate school and the field of MFT. During my undergraduate experience, at a predominantly White institution (PWI), I had explored my racial identity in relation to being Black, and had participated in and been accepted by the very small Black community on campus. While my racial identity was not solidified during that time (because as I mentioned I believe it is a lifelong process), I had gained so much from those interactions and experiences. During undergrad was the first time I was accepted as a person-of-color, prompting me to assert that identity more explicitly. However, I would not really start to explore the complexities of what it meant to be mixed race socially, until I started researching, reading about, and writing about the mixed-race experience as a graduate student. Digging into the literature and finding articles and books that reflected and expanded my own story opened up a world of virtual connection—the reality that there were other people like me, navigating the world from a unique racial identity.

In School

As I think about my post-secondary education, I know that one of the most important classes I ever took in undergrad was a sociology course titled *Racial Inequality*. It would be the first college course to open my eyes to the concepts of racism and inequality far beyond my own personal exposure and experiences. Additionally, it was the only time I have had an academic course taught by a Black male. That class and the deep, intense discussions about race had a profound impact on me—because others in that class and the professor saw me as one of the very few people of color, and while I did not fully comprehend it at the time, it also exposed me to the concept and effects of White privilege in American society. As I shared earlier, it was my journey in Biracial identity development during college that started me on the pathway to developing my sense of social location; but I did not have those words or understanding then.

As I reflect on my coursework and classes during my master's program, I do not recall an overt focus or integration of sociocultural awareness or consideration of diversity in therapy. I do recall a single class that focused on Diversity, yet the content of that course escapes me; which may speak to its ineffectiveness or my then lack of understanding of the critical nature of considering diversity in our work with clients. Whatever the reason, it did not have a significant impact on my way of thinking about or doing therapy at the time. It was actually in a theories class, where I was exposed to postmodernism and social constructionism that the importance of "diversity" factors started to come to the forefront. In particular, I remember learning about Michael White's concept of "the personal is political." Following that was my research class that provided me the freedom me to explore a topic I was personally interested in, that allowed me to consider the significance of a multiracial identity; more specifically my multiracial identity. My research professor provided feedback on my paper that changed my trajectory. It was her feedback, emphasizing the importance of the topic I had written about, that encouraged me to pursue doctoral work. I knew at the time what I was writing about was important to me, but I did not know that it could be important to others or even to the field of marriage and family therapy. This is yet another example of me minimizing my voice and keeping quiet about my lived experiences, because I felt in the minority. Moving forward I was reminded by my postmodern professor of how important each of our unique experiences and stories are, and how critical it is to create space for those stories (voices) to be heard and understood.

During my doctoral program, I worked with a professor who operated from a postmodern and feminist framework. She integrated these ideas into the classes she taught and encouraged us to integrate these frameworks in our clinical work as well. At the time, I was still really trying to navigate my sense of *imposter syndrome* being in a doctoral program, so those frameworks peripherally influenced my clinical work and my development as a therapist. My doctoral cohort was amazing, but I was the only person of color and we were located at a PWI in a predominantly White part of the state. I did not always feel comfortable talking about or bringing up my struggles about race and racial identity as a therapist-in-training—though I did keep writing and researching about it with a lot of support from my predominantly white professors and mentors.

Clinical Training Experience

My clinical training experience was both enriching and complex. I found my clinical calling during my traineeship to work with those who were dying and those who were grieving. My traineeship connected me with amazing colleagues with whom I established meaningful relationships. We supported and built each other up as people and as therapists. I learned the value of being myself while at my field site, and my self-of-the-therapist growth was also nurtured by two amazing supervisors. I worked with peers and others who had been in the field for years, while serving clients of various ages and socioeconomic backgrounds. Most of my mentors and peers were female, and all of my supervisors were White females, and the vast majority of my colleagues and clients were White. We did not discuss race, gender, or other aspects of identity as a part of our work and at the time I did not yet understand how important that was for me or my clients! Looking back, I do not fault those growth supporting supervisors for leaving those discussions out; I truly believe that at the time they were not trained in or aware of ways to integrate those conversations into supervision. I also think, with a group of predominantly white supervisees serving predominantly white clients, the importance of such conversations may not have seemed relevant.

While in my master's program, both at my field site and in my fieldwork class at school I also experienced supervisory relationships that were growth prohibiting. Because I was still developing my confidence that I did, in fact, belong in graduate school and that I could be and was a good therapist, those unsupportive supervisors had a significant impact on me. Those negative experiences, with people designated to help guide my growth, actually stunted me which led to my own self-silencing and feelings of inadequacy. Upon reflection, I am not sure that the supervisor or fieldwork instructor, both older White women and many years into their careers, knew how much power and destructive influence they had in my development. However, because I had not learned how to advocate for myself and did not quite believe that I was graduate school material, I internalized their negative feedback and unsupportive demeanors as confirmation that I did not belong. I know that if those negative experiences had not been balanced with positive supervisor and peer experiences, I would not have continued into this career. I now understand how critical the supervisor's role is in the development of the therapist's whole self and I am so thankful to the supervisors who did support me and for my inner strength in order to overcome self-doubt and get me through those early years.

A theme in my life experience is that of knowing who I am as a racial being but not always being seen or accepted as one. This is not necessarily a unique experience, but it is something that stands out as unique for me among people in my life. As a Biracial individual, during graduate school and during my career in higher education my awareness of being an "invisible" racial minority came to the forefront. As I mentioned previously, race and identity were not intimately discussed in either of my training programs for MFT, but my experiences related to my "invisible" racial identity in the therapy room stirred during both programs. It was during sessions with clients that I first experienced feeling invisible. Early in my training I encountered a client who made racist remarks about Black people, an indication that she did not see me as Black. I did not say anything to my client, my supervisor, or my colleagues. I said nothing, because I was not sure how to talk about it. It happened again during my doctoral program with another client, only this time I was being observed by my White, male peer supervisor. I did not say anything to the client, but my supervisor asked me about it after the session. I remember not knowing what to say about it, but feeling hurt, offended, and confused by my client. This was the first time a supervisor had considered my race in relation to therapy and at the time, and feeling overwhelmed, I never followed up with him. Like the first incident, this second incident stayed with me. It wouldn't be for years to come that I would learn how to talk about what had happened in those sessions—to apply concepts like microaggressions and oppression to my own experiences.

Raising of Critical Consciousness (Jessica)

I (Jessica) had been in a long-term and long-distance relationship throughout the master's program, while I worked for a few years, and as I began the doctoral program. From the beginning of that relationship, I was the "wrong" Asian ethnicity and my boyfriend's parents did not accept our dating and said things like they would disown him if he stayed with me. In my naivete, I thought that since we were all Christian, they would eventually change their minds and hearts because Christian values did not discriminate against people because of their racial or ethnic background. Certainly God would change perspectives if we all continued to be faithful. My sheltered Asian American Christian world at that point in time only knew a faith with clear outcomes. Additionally, I believed that God wanted me to be in this relationship and so I needed to be faithful, trusting, and committed, even if it got difficult.

Couples Research Group

From the start of the doctoral program, I was part of a weekly couples research group led by my professors, Dr. Carmen Knudson-Martin and Dr. Douglas Huenegardt. Every week the team of doctoral students and faculty would see couples in therapy—two people would be the co-therapists and the rest of us were observing through a one-way mirror. Looking at gender and power was the focus of our observations and clinical work. I remember wrestling with the concepts, as though there was a haze over my ability to comprehend the discussions. It was the feeling that there was a steep learning curve and that I could not grasp the ideas and was walking in a dimly lit room.

There was a long, dramatic, and traumatic end to the relationship, but an interesting thing happened afterward. Suddenly, all of the research and discussion about gender and power made sense to me. Something shifted—no longer feeling the gender-based powerlessness from being in the relationship—that allowed me to absorb (more like devour) the ideas. What ensued were three more years of researching gender, power, and culture which forever changed my life. There was much unpacking to do—reflecting on what kept me in the relationship so long, on my parents' relational dynamics, around cultural and religious ideas of gender and power. Deconstructing these core parts of our lives is never easy and I am grateful for the weekly support space to talk and theorize through my clinical and personal growth.

Much of the praise and affirmation I had received up until that point in life had to do with my accomplishments mixed with my being deferential, dutiful, compliant. For the first time, I felt increased permission to have access to the parts of me that could be opinionated, outspoken, and have a distinct perspective from others. I was experiencing my own contextual differentiation: developing conscious awareness of the influence of gendered power allowed me to choose how to engage in new ways in my context.

Engagement with White Faculty and Colleagues

It is a strange thing to reflect back on my life and to remember the tense energy I grew accustomed to holding when I was with White authority figures. Until now, I never reflected on how the majority of my teachers from kindergarten through twelfth grade were what I assumed to be White. I had one Japanese American algebra teacher in middle school, and a Korean American trigonometry teacher in high school. Our White teachers were teaching a largely immigrant and second-generation Asian American student population. I can still remember the way I felt especially with the White male teachers. They were kind and also expected much of the Asian American students (we were assumed to be high achieving) and I also experienced them as physically large and towering over me—it did not feel threatening, but it was intimidating. It's hard to pinpoint, but I remember wanting to please, impress them, and gain their approval.

From my pre-teen years through the end of college, my inner world was made up of other Asian American friends and families. The exterior world—teachers, professors, other authority figures—were White. They were the ones evaluating me, giving me my grades, comparing me to my peers (ranking us by grades) so it makes sense that I had to learn how to excel in the system they established for me, for us.

Fast forward to the start of my doctoral education. I did not know how to relate to my majority White classmates as peers. There was always a sense of being on the outside. I now know that I was used to living life code switching—accustomed to the unconscious energy exerted to fit in. Through our class discussions and readings around power and marginalization, we moved together in raising our shared critical consciousness. I began to identify and give language to my code switching and shared it with my professors and classmates. This of course, could not have happened without the sense of safety fostered by faculty and contributed to by peers.

In the classroom, peers began to pay attention to the experiences of racial/ethnic minority classmates and made room for our voices and stories. I still remember a class conversation where I had a comment to make but had a hard time finding the right space to interject and speak up. An older White male classmate noticed this and graciously created space for me. He checked in with me to see if this felt okay with me; it was a gesture that I appreciated.

Most of my PhD cohort were White women. When we spent time outside of the classroom, they started to notice the ways in which I was treated differently. Experiencing their interest and care in "my world" meant a great deal to me. These years together increased my contextual differentiation around racial dynamics and moved me toward being able to better identify and respond to racial interactions, particularly around whiteness.

Among the many faculty I interacted with during this season, three of my White professors/supervisors had a particularly significant impact on my self-awareness and growth. In my weekly supervision of supervision meetings, my clinical supervisor, an older White man, postured himself with such an openness and genuine interest in understanding my cultural background, and elicited my clinical perspective about how to do this or that. I had never been in a professional relationship where the supervisor positioned them self in a collaborative manner. I could feel myself having greater access to my own voice, cultural strengths, and clinical courage. Another professor, a White woman I respected, told me that I had great writing skills after I wrote my first literature review. This was deeply meaningful because I had grown up believing and being told that my writing would never be as good as my White "American" counterparts. Because of my relationship with this professor, I submitted my first conference proposal and developed enough confidence to consider the possibility of writing for publication. The third professor was my dissertation chair and advisor, an expert on gender and power in the MFT world. Once I started to speak up in our weekly couples research meetings, I remember the surprise and delight I felt when she genuinely wanted to learn something from me and my perspective on culture and race. I felt as though I had something to contribute and who I was mattered to our group. I am grateful for this mentorship that supported me through the writing and publication of several manuscripts and helped me land my first tenure-track faculty position.

Friendship with Queer Colleague

When I started the doctoral program, my world and reality was very heteronormative and had undercurrents of homophobia. I had gay friends in college but my "view" on sexuality was informed by a binary construct of gender and sexuality from my conservative Christian upbringing. A classmate, who was becoming a good friend, came out to me while we were students. I remember she was nervous about it and I could understand why, given her experiences with other evangelical people and institutions.

At that point in our friendship, we had been having conversations about race. I felt a sense of safety with this White friend because she modeled a humility, a genuine curiosity, and I witnessed her seeing and caring about the world with my experience in mind. There was a particular type of space we were cultivating in our connection—one of openness, assumption of positive intentions of the other, suspension of judgment, attending to discomfort and tension. So when she came out to me, I knew that I had a road ahead of me—one where I had to really examine my beliefs, assumptions, biases, judgments—about gender and sexuality.

I believe something about my experience of Christian faculty during my master's program allowed me to walk forward on this road. Their modeling of having open minds, hearts, and hands was the opposite of a position of fear (fear of questioning/losing faith) that I was accustomed to experiencing from religious communities. Those few years catalyzed a deconstruction of the various types of privilege in my own identity and context, and in the same way I experienced this friend choosing to walk alongside me around racial issues, I wanted her to feel and know that I deeply cared about her identity and being. My perspectives, beliefs, and theology have shifted along the way and I am grateful for the new communities of support and connection I have found that have allowed for this expansion and ongoing checking in with myself regarding gender identity and sexual orientation.

Working Alongside Colleagues of Color

The truth is that I had never heard of the term "people of color" until I was a doctoral student. I knew I needed to better understand my being a person of color and to connect with other people of color. At a national conference, I joined the people of color group, thinking it would be a space of feeling connected, seen, and encouraged. I actually felt very tense and uncomfortable during the meeting. I vaguely remember that there was frustration and anger in the group regarding experiences of being people of color and discussion about how to address these frustrations. I remember feeling pressured, intimidated, and alone. I felt like I had to use my voice in the way that these other leaders did—to be loud, unapologetic, and forceful. This was in direct opposition to anything I had ever been socialized or raised to be. I left confused and feeling as though I did not belong with the other people of color.

Over time, I started to pick up on my own experience of the in-betweenness that Asian Americans often feel regarding whiteness and blackness. In white spaces, I had already learned the social norms and expectations about how to carry myself; I had to be the one to adapt. In black and brown spaces, I often felt like I had to position myself one-down because of the honorary whiteness attributed to me. Curiosity or conversation about Asian American issues (or about me) was not common. This made it lonely and I often felt unseen in many of the diversity training and minority support workshops I attended.

I began to understand the privilege in the color of my skin—lighter East Asian American skin—and how it would never make me feel like a physical threat in certain contexts. But in some other spaces, my foreign-looking face, my "orientalness," could elicit disgust and hatred, never making me certain of my own safety.

What these experiences shaped in me is the recognition of the constant tensions that exist in our intersectional identities. How I experience myself, how others perceive me, what is expected of me, what discourses I want to live beyond, who I am becoming—it is a lot to navigate.

Raising of Critical Consciousness (Dana)

My Teaching and Supervision

It wasn't really until I started teaching, as a pre-doctoral intern at a PWI in Oregon, that I began to realize how important it was to be able to talk about my own identity (as person of color) and how it could not be separated from my work as a therapist. It was my students—the few students of color (and other marginalized statuses) in the program—who reached out to me as the only faculty of color, and brought it to my attention. During my second year of teaching, I was approached by a student who was one of very few males and one of the few students of color. This student was seeking a safe space to process and talk about his experiences of being a male therapist of color in the therapy room with his clients. He wanted to talk about how his clients experienced him and how he experienced his clients. In retrospect, I realized this student was in search of the exact tools I had both needed and lacked while I was a student and trainee. I came to realize through the sharing of his experiences, he could not separate or stop thinking about his identity as it intersected with his work with his clients, colleagues, and supervisors. At the time I did not yet have phrases like "critical consciousness" or "social location" to guide me or my student. However, I did have my own experiences to draw from along with my intuition as a therapist and person of color to begin creating space for those critical conversations to take place with that initial student and all those students who would follow.

In the years since that first student reached out to me, my own self-awareness and awareness of the experiences of others has steadily increased and more of my students who have marginalized statuses have shared with me how they have experienced microaggressions and slights from peers, professors, supervisors, and even clients. I have been intentional about creating space for students who may feel like they are the "only one" of a certain identity or experience to check in with me if they feel comfortable doing so. I am also purposeful to create an atmosphere in my classrooms and supervision groups that allows for difficult dialogues about social location among students to be shared and explored.

Being Seen as a Person of Color

My journey into the field of MFT added a significant component to my Biracial identity. As mentioned earlier, it was my research course instructor in my graduate program, an Asian female professor, who read my research proposal about Biracial Identity development and told me that even as a topic relatively unexplored at the time, it deserved continued research. I held onto her feedback and took my idea right into my doctoral program with the intent of formulating it further into my dissertation topic. I was successful in my dissertation proposal and began my qualitative research study, with the goal of interviewing Black-White Biracial families about racial identity and socialization. My journey into the stories and lives of 10 White mothers and 11 of their Biracial children changed my life. It was the first time that I had met other people like me with families like mine. It was the first time I felt truly understood and I wasn't even doing the talking! The experience of interviewing Biracial adults and their mothers validated so many of my own life experiences. And, I started to recognize that who I was and how I experienced the world as a racial being was, in fact, influenced by dominant discourses about single racial categories and what it means to be a light skinned woman of color. I also came to understand that the complexities of the stories of people like me needed to become a part of the discussions our culture was having about race in America ... and in the field of MFT. One gift of my research was the validation of my experience and then the impetus for sharing those stories through continued research, publication, and presentations. One disadvantage of my research was the requirement that I forfeit those connections with my research participants because of the nature of the researcher–participant relationship.

What is clear to me now, that was not clear then, was that I was coming into an understanding of my own social location and context. My social location as a Biracial woman and first-generation graduate student started to become centered as I was traversing the world of graduate school and developing my professional identity. Jessica coined the term contextual differentiation. It turns out, that I was becoming contextually differentiated—in my experiences up to that point, I had struggled with feeling incompetent and silenced, unsure that what I was thinking and feeling was significant. The dominant discourses that had rendered doubt in my mind were slowly getting deconstructed and replaced with louder and more powerful local discourses and preferred narratives that validated me.

As I continued to increase confidence in my sense of self, I began using my voice more, to represent another perspective of the marginalized experience related to race and gender in my work. I started sharing my experiences and how I navigated the world as a person of color with my students and then eventually with my (mostly White) colleagues as well. In turn, I found others (students, as mentioned before, and colleagues) coming to me to engage in dialogue and asking for advice, guidance, or support, and they were also sharing their stories. It was at my current job, as a full-time faculty member that I began establishing more transparent and forthcoming relationships with other women of color, specifically Jessica, and two colleagues (outside of MFT) who identify as Black. The relationships I have nurtured with these two colleagues are open, honest, and mutually supportive. It is the first time in my life that I can engage about anything and everything related to race, gender, and being Biracial with Black female peers. I understand now that feeling seen and heard as a person of color by women who identify as Black has been a critical component of finding my voice and allowed me to move into yet another phase of my identity as a Biracial woman. It has also been within those relationships that I have been able to acknowledge and discuss injustices centered in race as well as my light skin privilege and the differences in how we experience the world and our Blackness.

Building Community

Mentorship

As a doctoral student, against all structural expectations, I intentionally chose an early career female professor who was similar in age to me to chair my dissertation. I remember when I first met her, feeling inspired by her accomplishments in the field at what I perceived as a young(ish) age. She started teaching in my doctoral program the same year I started as a student. She was both astute and caring. Since I left Virginia to enter my pre-doctoral internship in Oregon before I completed my dissertation, I needed to lean on her for guidance and support from a long distance (this was before the ease of cell phones, texting, and video chatting). In some ways I think we supported each other through that time, since I know I was her first official doctoral graduate student to complete the program under her direction. She was inspirational to me for so many reasons and I will forever be grateful to her as an example of what I could hope to be as a future professor.

Friendships

Another significant component of my journey as a person of color in the field of MFT relates to building community both within the field and just outside of it. It started in my graduate program, breaking out of my shell and establishing relationships with a few wonderful women with whom I studied and traveled to my first conference, and one of whom I have remained close to even though we have lived long distances apart for the greater part of our friendship. It was she with whom I learned the ropes of being an MFT, with whom I dove deeper into narrative therapy, and whom I turned to for support during our different doctoral programs. During my time in my doctoral program I established a special bond with the other two women in my cohort. We connected on an interpersonal and deep level as women of varying identities navigating the competitive world of PhDs. Together we grew in our knowledge about the field of MFT and together we resisted the cutthroat nature of academia and supported each other in finding our own career paths.

Support Group

Just a few years ago, with the help of a social justice-oriented peer, I found the Critical Mixed Race Studies (CMRS) conference. It was at this conference that I was introduced to a world of research centered in the mixed-race experience and I was introduced to a wide world of mixed-race people! At the first CMRS conference I attended I made a decision to meet people I found interesting and to start conversations about my research interests or theirs to build connections. I gathered business cards and contact information and within weeks of returning from the conference made the decision to reach out to some of those women. My life has forever been changed! I now have a support group of Biracial women—we are from different disciplines—but we share a sacred space as co-researchers, accountability partners, and enthusiastic friends.

My Reflections (Dana)

My continued education and growth related to the concepts and ideas in Chapter 1 are informed by my connections with colleagues, like Jessica (and many more mentioned in Chapter 8), who teach me what they know and who engage in discussions and who make recommendations for readings, activities, and workshops. I also continue to learn and expand my knowledge through my reading literature and research, both academic and colloquial, by attending workshops, trainings, and presentations; and teaching about these topics in my MFT program with my students. I have been in the field of marriage and family therapy for over 16 years as a clinician and 14 years teaching and providing clinical supervision. I am currently a full-time professor and clinical supervisor in a COAMFTE-accredited marriage and family therapy graduate program at California State University, Northridge. To serve others as a teacher, supervisor, and mentor is a privilege. To bear witness to and learn from the intimate stories of my clients, students, and colleagues is truly a gift. I am a lifelong learner, committed to my own growth and development in relationships, personally and professionally.

Becoming Colleagues and Friends

I (Jessica) started a tenure-track faculty position as an assistant professor of MFT at California State University, Northridge (CSUN) the fall after I graduated from the PhD program. From the time that I met Dana, I knew that she was someone with warmth, kindness, and hospitality. There were many points of connection for us that, in looking back now, I believe gave me a sense of trust about deepening the working relationship with her. We talk about civility and trust later in the book (Chapter 7) and my relationship with Dana is a wonderful example of a collegial relationship that began with a good foundation of civility and trust-building capacity. When I interviewed for the position, I had made it known that I cared about diversity, equity, and social justice and that gave Dana information about me that she could move toward. From that point on, there was always a flow to our friendship. We would talk about everything and very quickly, issues of sociocultural context were part of those conversations.

I (Dana) had been at CSUN for three years before Jessica came. I was adjusting to and establishing relationships, engrossed in my teaching and mentoring my students, but I had yet to find my voice as a faculty of color and to share my ideas about diversity, equity, and social justice. Then we interviewed Jessica! From the first contact with her, something in me came alive. She brought up her equity mindedness, social justice orientation, and her values about diversity in every conversation. I was convinced that she would be an awesome fit for our students and with our faculty. Jessica said it already, and I concur, the initial connection we made over those shared values ushered me into yet another phase of finding my voice and using it as an educator and faculty member. Jessica has served as a mentor and a sounding board for me in my teaching as well as in my own personal growth and development.

In our respective contexts, we shared the experience of in-betweenness, with Asian American identity and Biracial identity. This, along with our collaborative personalities, set the stage for the following years of preparing for and teaching courses (such as the "diversity" course) together, debriefing painful or challenging dynamics with students, championing equity in our program and department, and going to consciousness-raising workshops and trainings. Even though Jessica is no longer teaching at CSUN, we value the relationship we cultivated and continue to grow together. This book was written while we were geographically close as much as it was written while we were far apart.

Summary

Our voices are just part of the countless narratives from our field. We appreciate you taking the time to read our narratives and how we began the journey of raising critical consciousness in our lives. As we wrote our stories, we recognized that while we were going through various experiences, we did not have the awareness nor did it feel cohesive. It is in retrospect now that we are able to construct our narratives in ways that make sense to us. We continue to walk on the path towards consciousness raising and hope that we have encouraged you to consider your own journey. In the following two chapters, we offer a review of the literature regarding difficult and meaningful/fulfilling experiences in MFT education and training so that you can be familiar with this literature but also locate your experiences within the wider community.

> **Questions for Reflection**
>
> 1. Are there parts of Dana's or Jessica's narratives you resonate with? React to? Wonder about?
> 2. What does the season of dysconsciousness look like in your life? What allowed it to remain that way?
> 3. What has contributed and/or is contributing to the raising of consciousness in your life? People? Contexts? Resources? Life experiences?
> 4. Who are some people, what are some communities/groups that you can reach out to for support as you continue through this book?

References

King, J. E. (1991). Dysconscious racism: Ideology, identity, and the miseducation of teachers. The *Journal of Negro Education*, 60(2), 133–146.

Yu, K. (2016). Christian model minority: Racial and ethnic formation in Asian American Evangelicalism. *Journal of Race, Ethnicity, and Religion*, 7(4), 1–24.

Difficult and Unfulfilling Training Experiences 3

Being a trainee in any field comes with its fair share of challenges and growth experiences. Inherent to any growth and development process is the experience of being stretched, pushed, and shaped by circumstances and people. Growth experiences can be helpful, healthy, and intentional (learning to work with colleagues, difficult clinical cases, intervening in trauma/crises); they can also be unexpected, a result of unintentional or intentional harm or pain (unjust institutions, biases in colleagues, etc.). In this chapter, we want to speak to the difficult and unfulfilling training experiences that are a result of the latter: when MFT trainees face hurtful or even traumatic interactions.

We have had our share of challenging training experiences as supervisees and over the years as we have talked with students and colleagues, we have learned that this is not uncommon. This chapter is not meant to cast supervisors or the field in a negative light. Our intention for this chapter is twofold. First, we hope that it affirms and validates trainees, interns, and supervisees. Some trainees may currently be experiencing challenges and we want you to know you are not alone. Others may be students anticipating the start of an MFT graduate program or looking for their first clinical placement site. We hope this literature and the case examples give you wisdom for the path forward.

Our other intention for this chapter is to speak to those of us who are educators, supervisors, and those who provide supervision training. The field of marriage and family therapy is hopefully continuing to move toward diversifying our therapist population and as we do so, our role as supervisors is to understand how to best connect with, support, and train our supervisees. Therapists with marginalized identities of any kind are most likely to be missed because regardless of the supervisor's social location, the majority of us have been trained and educated in White male heteronormative systems. This informs our communication styles, expectations, and assumptions about what a "good therapist" looks like and thus influences our supervision trajectories. May we allow this research and these stories to challenge and grow us.

Why Trainees' Experiences Matter

We recognize that MFT training occurs in multiple settings, some of which are large systems and it is certainly a challenge for educators and supervisors to be intimately aware of each trainee's unique experience. While it may not be realistic to know the ins and outs of each trainee's experience, we believe and assume that those of us who are educators and supervisors value our students and trainees as they are the foundation of our field. They are often the ones navigating some of the hardest crises and touching the lives of some of the most marginalized client populations.

We are directly involved in and responsible for their training and growth experiences. There is isomorphism on many levels in our field: how we interact with our trainees shapes their interactions with clients, and how we interact with trainees influences their future interactions with supervisees. There is much power inherent in the role of the supervisor and educator. Who we are, the values we intentionally or unintentionally share, and our actions contribute to the experiences of our trainees and to the culture and reality of our field.

Embedded in Systems

Many dynamics shape the trainee experience. Of course there are the individual dyadic relationships: those with clients, supervisors, and colleagues. Then there are larger structural influences such as the programs and departments within academic institutions or clinical placement sites and the funding agencies and organizations with which they are associated. Difficult and unfulfilling training experiences can be connected to any one or multiple parts of these systems. We will address these experiences from the larger institutional levels down to the dyadic relationships.

Experiences within Systems

While our education trains us to think systemically, it is easy to miss the systemic nature of our academic or clinical experiences. There are of course amazing supervisors and educators as well as those that are not as good. In this section we want to highlight the connection that institutions have to the culture of programs and work settings as well as to the individuals that are hired to become part of such systems. We will look at specific dyadic relationships later; here we hope to highlight the significance of being curious about the systems within which we choose to work or study. Often times, the decisions and agendas of these larger structures influence the specific individual experiences that students and trainees have.

MFT Training Institutions

The location and geographical context of schools and placement settings has much of an influence on the experience of students and trainees. Universities can have mission statements that reflect values of social justice, but the question is if the staff and faculty, student body, and policies reflect such values. Additionally, a question to ask is how much is the university engaging with the community within which it is embedded and critically examining how to engage with and serve those communities?

Location

When we discuss location, we are thinking about the diversity of the community and how this intersects with the institution's setting (rural or urban, private or public, etc.). Mittal and Wieling (2006) interviewed 13 international MFT doctoral students studying in the U.S. Six of the participants shared that the location of their university had an impact on their training experiences.

> Three participants emphasized the awareness of people about their country's culture, friendliness, and ethnic and cultural diversity in

the population as having a positive impact on their graduate school experiences. Three other participants reported negative experiences due to a lack of cultural diversity and the populations' unfamiliarity with different ethnic groups.

(p. 374)

For the first three participants, when the community members knew about their country of origin, were friendly, and there was ethnic diversity—this led to positive experiences. When the community did not have cultural diversity (representation), the other three participants had negative experiences. When a community appreciates difference, racial/ethnic minority students have fewer microaggressions and overt racist experiences. It contributes to a general sense of feeling welcomed and less like an outsider. These types of experiences do not belong only to international students. When people in the community surrounding a school, the university students, or a clinic's client population do not reflect the identities of the MFT student/trainee, feelings of being different naturally arise. Individuals with marginalized identities are typically already acutely aware of how they are different or do not fit into dominant contexts; this is often exacerbated by the experience of microaggressions that reinforce how foreign, different, unknown or unseen the student is because of some attribute of their identity. Having this daily experience is certain to affect the student's sense of self and can be physically and emotionally exhausting. Here is the experience of a queer student in a religious institution, sharing about how the institutional structure and unspoken rules impacted her development.

Voice of a Student

All of my education beyond high school took place within private evangelical universities. At an undergraduate level, this was a wonderful experience, something I chose and felt very grateful for. Although this was before I began to have a sense of my own queer identity. Over time, as this aspect of my identity came more and more to the fore, the more challenging the larger evangelical influence became for me within the universities I attended. As a doctoral student in marriage and family therapy, the religiosity of the institution seemed to create a double-bind for me in terms of both my academic and personal development. Let me explain. In the field of family therapy we are encouraged to do what one might call, "self" work. Which is to say, we are given the directive to explore how our families of origin have impacted and shaped us, and to examine how those early learnings and relationships continue to influence how we work with clients and situate ourselves in the social world. We are also encouraged to explore the intersectional aspects of our own identities, specifically examining how these parts of ourselves inform, in part, how we understand the world around us, how we engage in relationship with colleagues and clients, what we attend to in our surrounding environment, and what we don't. This goes even further to investigating how our identities have worked together to produce bias and assumptions we might hold about those like us, and those different from us. The challenge in this for me as a queer doctoral student at a religious institution was that I was not encouraged to integrate my queerness into these formative queries of how my identities had led me to piece my world together. In fact, I was explicitly encouraged to be cautious about my queerness and to not speak of it in a public way, which meant that even in a class assignment on constructing one's own personal narrative around privilege and oppression, I was strongly advised to focus on other parts of my identity and experience that did not include who I was as a queer person. This not only seemed contradictory, but it inhibited me from being able to develop a deeper understanding of how my queerness played a role in making me who I am, the experiences I have had, and how all that related to my development as a therapist. A central component of family therapy training is whole person development. This is generally accompanied by helping students gain a greater capacity for self- reflection and reflexivity, an understanding of their various social identities and the meaning those carry in terms how they relate to those around them. As a student, I wasn't able to do that when it came to my own queerness. So while I was being told to develop and reflect in all these ways, I was also implicitly being limited in how far of a reach that development could take place. This has meant that I have had to do a lot of "thinking through" things beyond my doctoral education, which I hope is what we all do beyond our degrees, although it was a very difficult experience to have had to minimize one of the best parts of my life and aspects of my identity. Many of the best things in my life are directly because I am queer, not in spite of it.

It may not be realistic to expect that every institution will have a diverse student or staff population. However, in places with more homogeneity, without intentional critical consciousness, institutions absorb values and interests that reflect that of the dominant culture. It takes more concerted effort, planning, and preparation to examine how the context and location shape the learning and experiences of students, for both marginalized students and those with dominant identities. Without intentional action-oriented effort at institutional levels, students can experience painful exclusion and trauma.

Culture of and Accountability within Departments, Programs, and Clinics

Though the location of a university or clinic may not have the most diverse population, departments, programs, and clinics can still be thriving places where all students feel seen and treated with equity and respect.

A department or clinic's policies, particularly how and whom they hire and how they maintain accountability for their equity practices, are critical to the health of the students and staff. Though indirect, such policies and procedures can contribute to students having difficult, wonderful, or challenging training experiences. How clearly does the department value and uphold anti-discrimination and inclusion of all community members? How are staff and faculty trained, held accountable, and supported to live out such values?

I (Jessica) felt supported as a female assistant professor of color when I was one of the full-time faculty in an MFT program; I felt the support across multiple levels—from colleagues, the department chair, college dean, and the larger university administration. The campus regularly hosted events that supported junior faculty of color, keeping us connected to and aware of the needs of our predominantly racial minority and immigrant student population. The leadership in the college and department modeled accountability for their own growth in critical consciousness and facilitated dialogue and check-ins with faculty when current events impacted the campus; they made sure that faculty were attended to and that they were also attending to the needs of the students. The message I received was that our university, college, and department valued the ongoing growth and well-being of faculty so that we could best serve a diverse student population. I also sensed that the campus community understood that such work was not easy and that regular dialogue and assessment was needed for continued advancement. I am aware that this sort of experience is not the norm and have heard countless stories from peers at other universities who felt isolated or invisible in their efforts toward justice or discouraged because of not having the support to engage in critical pedagogy.

To whatever degree a department, program, or clinic values diversity, equity, and inclusion, support for training around such issues is critical (Jackson, 1999). Piercy and colleagues (2016) surveyed 68 students and graduates of COAMFTE-accredited master's or doctoral programs to understand their most and least meaningful couple and family therapy learning experiences. One theme that surfaced under least meaningful experiences was "Lack of Diverse Perspectives." A number of participants discussed classes lacking cultural inclusivity and sensitivity. One participant shared about an unhelpful professor of a multicultural course who was "more focused on discussing some of his own experiences and was very biased in his approach" (p. 592). It is important for programs to listen closely to the experiences and feedback of students, particularly around multicultural/diversity courses and content, and to consider how faculty contribute to shaping the culture and inclusion of all students.

The makeup of the faculty and supervisors influences student experience as well. Prouty, Helmeke, and Fischer (2016) surveyed 293 students and graduates of COAMFTE-accredited programs to understand their experiences of mentorship. They affirmed previous research findings that "graduate students felt that the quality of the mentorship provided from people similar to themselves was better" (p. 49) and so they encourage continuing the practice of hiring "faculty and senior clinicians of all genders, ethnic and sexual minorities, and from many countries, and provide diversity sensitivity training" (p. 49). It would benefit the field and profession to deepen the quality of mentor and mentees' experiences by increasing accessibility to a diverse group of faculty and supervisors.

Dyadic Relationships

Supervisory Relationship

When we think about impactful training experiences, most seasoned clinicians recall the individual relationships we have had with supervisors and faculty in the field. When we think of the MFT training experience, the supervisory relationship is one of the most primary and foundational to this season of growth. There are a number of articles that speak to this.

Best and Worst Supervision Experiences

Anderson, Schlossberg, and Rigazio-DiGilio (2000) conducted a research study exploring MFT trainees' best and worst supervision experiences. While social location of the participants is not noted, with the exception of age (22 to 59 years of age) and gender (39% male, 61% female), the findings provide helpful insight. Forty-five American Association of Marriage and Family Therapy (AAMFT) COAMFTE-accredited programs participated. Here are some interesting general findings:

- Both best and worst experiences were likely to occur during a beginning practicum experience as opposed to a doctoral level internship
- It was almost twice as likely for trainees to have a worst experience at a community clinic (18%) than a best experience at one (10%)
- Group supervision was three times more likely to have been reported as a worst experience (29%) as opposed to a best experience (10%)
- Having the same supervisor for both individual supervision and group supervision was connected with best experiences
- Best experiences more commonly involved live supervision (35%) and worst experiences tended to rely on verbal report (38%)
- Worst experiences happened more often (10%) when the supervisor's primary role was that of an administrator. They contributed to best experiences only 1% of the time
- When a supervisor's primary orientation was behavioral, 13% were worst experiences vs. 1% were best experiences
- A notable finding is that two-thirds of worst experiences were reported to be with a male supervisor

There was one item selected by more than one-third of the participants that was an attribute of their worst experience: "students' weaknesses and shortcomings were emphasized" (Anderson, Schlossberg, & Rigazio-DiGilio, 2000, p. 86). Almost a third of participants also mentioned the supervisor's "heavy emphasis on evaluation," "encouraging unthinking conformity," and "intolerance for divergent viewpoints" (p. 86). This contrasts what trainees associated with their best experiences of supervision which was emphasizing personal growth instead of technical skills.

There were some factors that were not significant in shaping best or worst experiences such as some contextual variables like training setting, the client population, and the supervisor's professional role or experience level. However, a few factors set apart best experiences such as trainees rating supervisors as "more interpersonally attractive (friendly, likeable, sociable, warm), trustworthy, and expert" (Anderson, Schlossberg, & Rigazio-DiGilio, 2000, p. 88). Another factor contributing to best experiences was the greater amount and frequency of supervisor contact. "The best supervision experiences were significantly longer in duration, involved more hours of weekly contact between the supervisor and supervisee, and included discussion of a greater number of cases per session" (p. 89). Participants also had better experiences associated with more family and couples cases per week. This was more important than the supervisor's theoretical orientation or experience. These findings can inform programs in reflecting on how their supervisory dynamics are set up to maximize supervisee and supervisor connection.

Anderson and colleagues (2000) reported four notable dimensions highlighted by participants regarding best supervision characteristics.

> The first was a sense of openness in the supervisory environment. This was reflected in items that described supervisors as "welcoming mistakes as a part of the learning experience," being "open to feedback," "respecting value differences," "exploring new ideas and therapeutic techniques," and providing opportunities for "students to observe one another's work."
>
> A second dimension emphasized communicating respect, support, and encouragement. This was evident in such items as the supervisor's providing "praise and encouragement," "respecting the personal time demands of the supervisee," treating the supervisee "as a colleague," scheduling time "exclusively for supervision," and being "accessible outside the regular schedule."
>
> A third dimension emphasized the personal growth aspect of supervision, noted earlier in the analysis of mean differences between best and worst experiences. Items such as the supervisor's "encouragement of personal growth issues" and willingness to "directly confront supervisees' blind spots and resistances" reflected this dimension.
>
> A fourth dimension highlighted conceptual and technical guidance and direction. This dimension included the supervisor providing "useful conceptual frameworks for understanding clients," "feedback that was direct and straightforward," the "teaching of practical skills," and the supervisors' "demonstration of their own therapeutic skill".
>
> (p. 86)

Having a better understanding of supervisees' best and worst supervision experiences through Anderson and colleagues' (2000) study can support supervisors and programs to reflect on our own development as well as how we might shape clinical and programmatic structures to maximize best experiences for our students. Of course no two programs are the same so it would be beneficial to survey or systematically check in with students to seek their feedback about their supervision experiences.

Individual Supervision

Thirty-five second year full-time MFT students participated in a study that explored the daily events and emotions of family therapy trainees (Edwards & Patterson, 2012). Interestingly, individual supervision was rated as one of the top five least enjoyable training activities. This connects to what Anderson, Schlossberg, and Rigazio-DiGilio (2000) reported about how supervision is less enjoyable when trainees' shortcomings and weaknesses are the focus. On one hand, it is an important skill to learn to be able to hear and learn from critical feedback. However, individual supervision does not have to be a least enjoyable activity when we as supervisors thoughtfully consider how we are shaping trainees' experiences and how we are offering feedback. It is important to consider the unconscious ways that biases come out through critique and criticism. Do supervisors privilege a particular style or way of doing therapy? How might this be related to their own sociocultural context and could it be unfair to put this expectation on supervisees of different sociocultural backgrounds?

Inherent in the supervision relationship is power. As supervisors we hold power in that we are shaping the clinical and ethical foundations of our trainees and are often responsible for passing them onto the next stage of their licensing process. Not only is this common in the MFT field, but across other mental health disciplines, it is not easy or typical for conversations about power to be had in supervision. Meta-communication about the supervisory relationship is rare, meaning that talking about how the supervisory relationship is going is not common practice (Mangione et al., 2011). Often times, supervisees initiate these conversations, and not supervisors, particularly when there is a problem. It is more common for the supervisee to be aware of the power dynamic in supervision (since they are in a position of being evaluated) and supervisees would generally like to have more of these dialogues about power in the supervisory relationship. As supervisors model the appropriate use of power, they can empower trainees to do the same when they supervise and mentor in the future (Green & Dekkers, 2010).

Ethnic Minority Supervisors' Experiences as Supervisees

Hernández, Taylor, and McDowell (2009) conducted a qualitative study interviewing ten ethnic minority AAMFT-approved supervisors. The researchers sought to understand how the participants' own supervision experiences, during their training, influenced their role as supervisors, particularly in relation to when and how to bring up issues of diversity, how they hoped to impact supervisees, and supervisor training needs. The participants included nine females and one male, their ages ranged from 36 to 62, and one identified as bisexual and nine as heterosexual. The participants self-identified as Chicana, Puerto Rican, South Asian, Asian Chinese, Mixed (Native and European), African American, and Chinese and they reported their class background ranging between Lower Class and Upper Middle Class. All of the participants had been supervisors from four to 20 years; as supervisees, half had no personal experience with supervisors of color and at most some had one ethnic minority supervisor. As supervisors themselves, they had eight to 34 ethnic minority supervisees across the years.

Hernandez and colleagues (2009) reported three themes that emerged from these participants' experiences as supervisees: (1) lack of processing social location and diversity dimensions, (2) misuse of power by supervisors, and (3) lack of mentorship in the profession. These seem to have contributed to their difficult and/or unfulfilling training experiences.

When reflecting back on their experiences as supervisees, participants reported that their supervisors did not know how to address social location issues, especially how they influenced therapy and supervision (Hernández, Taylor, & McDowell, 2009). Such experiences affected the participants by making them much more aware when they became supervisors themselves in focusing on differing social locations in their role as supervisors. One participant shared:

> What really began to shape my supervision was my experience as a supervisee. Where it was very frustrating, although I had very good supervision in terms of the techniques, their ability to understand the intersectionality of difference was extremely poor. They had very little idea on how to look at the difference between a white therapist and a family of color.
>
> (p. 92)

The majority of participants shared this challenging experience of supervisors missing sensitivity and lacking expertise in processing difference. They also mentioned that the supervisor's ethnicity was not as important as if the supervisor had critical consciousness and an "awareness of the intersection of diversity issues and their impact on the therapeutic and supervisory relationships" (pp. 92–93). If diversity was discussed during supervision, participants reported that focus and depth were lacking. "A participant noted that social location was often discussed in a cursory fashion; people would name demographics or issues and maybe revert to stereotypical descriptions of them" (p. 93). A common experience of ethnic minority individuals was shared by these participants in that they held "the burden of representing their entire culture and were thought of as the expert for their ethnicity" (p. 93).

Hernandez and colleagues (2009) found that misuse of power was a second important theme reported by the participants from this study. While this may be surprising to some readers, it is unfortunately still a reality in many supervision experiences. Participants in the study experienced overt racism and ignorance as trainees. Racism was experienced as "unintentional interactions to overt, harmful statements and behaviors" (p. 95).

> Their supervisors made racist comments, showed preference to supervisees of their own ethnic class, were blind to diversity issues (especially sexual orientation and spirituality), or matched supervisors and supervisees based on their ethnicity, reflexively assuming that such matching is a good training practice in all instances.
>
> (p. 94)

Such experiences in dyadic supervision relationships are often interconnected to institutional realities, as participants referenced the male-dominated nature of their training experiences. Supervisors also misused power in not addressing diversity issues, which were often silenced or brought up only if initiated by the supervisee.

The third theme reported by the participants in the study was lack of mentorship in the profession (Hernández, Taylor, & McDowell, 2009). Just about all of the participants expressed not having supervisors within the field to mentor them professionally around their critical consciousness development. As a result, participants found mentors through looking to clients (one participant described learning from clients who were elders in the community by witnessing their stories), family members, and community members. Some of the participants in the study who eventually became educators themselves shared that they learned about issues of diversity from their students and through teaching more than through their supervision experiences. Hernández, Taylor, and McDowell (2009) reflected that these were the experiences of ethnic minority supervisees who chose to become approved supervisors and that there may be others who never completed their training as a result of such unfulfilling training experiences.

From these studies, we glean that the training of supervisors should include personal growth, self-of-the-supervisor awareness and development, intentional diversity, and critical consciousness raising in all training programs.

Peer and Colleague Relationships

In Supervision

Interactions with other trainees can elicit some of the most positive experiences in training (Edwards & Patterson, 2012). There can also be some painful experiences with peers and colleagues. In a qualitative study of eight MFT students or recent graduates exploring their racial experiences, some of the most difficult experiences were related to the negative stereotypes of others (McDowell, 2004). Experiencing differential treatment based on race was reported as subtle and unintentional. One participant shared about her experience with White peers:

> It was not obvious ... People were friendly and tried hard not to be discriminating. I felt the discrimination was very subtle. For example, if I was having a conversation with a group of White classmates, I just didn't feel that I was able to lead a topic, lead a conversation. My remarks weren't paid attention to. They were ignored. And then I just felt that I was always an outsider ...
>
> (p. 311)

Subtle and regular experiences like this can make it difficult for a trainee/student to feel like they belong and that they have something worthwhile to contribute to the program or the field.

In the Classroom

One of the few studies that surveyed family therapy students about their experience with class found that participants felt more marginalized by their peers than professors in regard to issues of class (McDowell et al., 2013). Of the 61 participants who self-identified as having grown up in lower or working-class families, "51.1% of respondents felt the need to hide or censor their social background and felt alienated from their peers at least some of the time" (p. 81). One participant shared:

> I hear comments from graduate students, who [talk] about how school is easy or how a person should already know how to do research. [These] comments make me want to shut down and not open up to the many struggles I have about being in a lower social class. The opportunities growing up were not there as they are for people in middle to upper classes.
>
> (p. 81)

As participants in this study expressed, it is all too easy to assume that students come from middle-class experiences and opportunities. Because identities like socioeconomic status and class have little outward indication, classmates can assume sameness with one another, thus leading to the silent alienation of those who do not fit such assumptions of being middle-class. This can magnify the experience of feeling like an outsider or an impostor. It is important for faculty and programs to be aware of the many facets of students' identities and to establish a community culture that is attuned and sensitive to all kinds of difference, visible or invisible.

Relationships with Clients

Rastogi and Wieling (2005) have an excellent book, *Voices of Color: First Person Accounts of Ethnic Minority Therapists* that speaks to many types of experiences that clinicians have, including experiences of racism in the therapy room. One particular chapter highlights the first-hand experiences of therapists in training.

One therapist of color shared about racism expressed by clients in a family therapy setting. She has heard comments such as "My mom and I were talking about how Mexican men are so loud and drunk all the time, not all of them, but most of them" (Ali et al., 2005, p. 120). A common response, as the therapist described, is for the therapist to become confused and vulnerable, wondering about why the clients would say this knowing that the therapist is a person of color. What also takes place is the inclination to make sense of the clients' behaviors by finding an explanation. The therapist is often left with a flood of thoughts and emotions and no actual explanation from the client.

Another supervisee who identified as a Biracial woman, half Filipino and half European American reported about her work with a 20-year-old White male; the client said "I'm so sick of minorities and women getting all the breaks. They get all the handouts while the rest of us have to work for what we get" (Ali et al., 2005, p. 121). This supervisee was overwhelmed by many thoughts and feelings, particularly anger and she wondered if the client knew her Biracial identity; was she White or Brown to him? In attempting to bring this issue up in supervision, the supervisor made assumptions about how the supervisee identifies and affirmed her ethnic minority identity while neglecting her White identity. This perpetuated the therapist not feeling seen, known, or having a sense of belonging.

A last example comes from an Asian American therapist who was working with White European American veterans. There was much self-talk and wondering that took place in the therapist's mind with questions such as "What will the Vietnam veterans see in me? Instead of the eager healer, will they see the 'enemy,' the 'foreigner,' or the 'person who will never be an American no matter how hard he tries'" (Ali et al., 2005, p. 126). Ethnic minority therapists carry internalized racism (Bivens, 1995) and their day-to-day lived experiences of racism into their therapy work. One of the veteran clients told stories about how he committed acts of violence on people that the therapist resembled. The therapist shared the following internal dialogue:

> How am I supposed to take this? Has my training covered this? What is appropriate professional behavior? Anger and fear rise up in my throat. My confidence in my skill is precarious. Surely a more competent therapist would be able to manage these feelings in session even in the face of this abuse ... I want to hide, blend in, and be invisible to defend myself from my client's racism ... Racism reminds me of how despite my higher education, and my middle-class values and aspirations, I reside inches from marginalization and what seems like miles from my client.
>
> (p. 126)

These are merely a few examples of how ethnic minority therapists have both covert and overt experiences of racism while in the therapy room. MFT programs and supervision settings must speak to these realities and provide the training and support to students so their experiences as therapists do not further traumatize or marginalize them. When experiences of racism while being the therapist remain unknown or not discussed with supervisors, ethnic minority therapists can begin to feel as though they do not belong in the profession, question their abilities, and feel even more isolated, overwhelmed, and stressed. We believe it is an ethical duty for our profession to directly speak to and provide culturally sensitive support to the marginalizing experiences students will inevitably face during their training.

Summary

In the MFT training experience, there are many settings in which hurtful and harmful interactions can take place: in dynamics with clients, supervisors, colleagues, as well as in academic programs embedded in departments and universities. Many of the studies we cited focused on racial and ethnic identity experiences. We hope you will take the time to look up newer research on the experiences of supervisees and students of different marginalized identities. For some of the readers, we hope this chapter validates the experiences you have had; for other readers we hope it allows you to see the experiences of some of your colleagues and students through the lens of the research and stories.

Questions for Reflection

1. If you have had a difficult training experience(s), what connection to issues of social location and relational power might it have had?
2. What critical feedback have you received that was difficult or hurtful to hear? Could this feedback be related to implicit biases on the part of the supervisor/professor? Are there helpful truths in the feedback that can help you grow personally and professionally?
3. Take some time to think about your peers and colleagues with various marginalized identities. Are there parts of their

experience you might be missing or unintentionally minimizing that is hard for you to recognize?
4. While ensuring you have an adequate support system and faculty/peer allies, and having considered any possibility of being harmed by the system, would it be helpful to address the issues related to your unsatisfactory training experience? Are there professionally appropriate levels of communication, such as first with a direct supervisor or professor, then the chair of a program/program director, so on and so forth? Are there support or advocacy groups that can advise or join you in these efforts?

References

Ali, S. R., Flojo, J. R., Chronister, K. M., Hayashino, D., Smiling, Q. R., Torres, D., & McWhirter, E. H. (2005).When racism is reversed: Therapists of color speak out about their experiences with racism from clients, supervisees, and supervisors. In M. Rastogi & E. Wieling (Eds.), *Voices of color: First-person accounts of ethnic minority therapists* (117–134). Thousand Oaks, CA: Sage.

Anderson, S. A., Schlossberg, M., & Rigazio-DiGilio, S. (2000). Family therapy trainees' evaluations of their best and worst supervision experiences. *Journal of Marital and Family Therapy, 26*(1), 79–91.

Bivens, D. (1995). Internalized racism: A definition. Retrieved from www.racialequitytools.org/resourcefiles/bivens.pdf

Edwards, T. M., & Patterson, J. E. (2012). The daily events and emotions of master's-level family therapy trainees in off-campus practicum settings. *Journal of Marital and Family Therapy, 38*(4), 688–696.

Green, M. S. & Dekkers, T. D. (2010). Attending to power and diversity in supervision: An exploration of supervisee learning outcomes and satisfaction with supervision. *Journal of Feminist Family Therapy, 22*(4), 293–312.

Hernández, P., Taylor, B. A., & McDowell, T. (2009). Listening to ethnic minority AAMFT approved supervisors: Reflections on their experiences as supervisees. *Journal of Systemic Therapies, 28*(1), 88–100.

Jackson, L. C. (1999). Ethnocultural resistance to multicultural training: Students and faculty. *Cultural Diversity & Ethnic Minority Psychology, 5*(1), 27–36.

Mangione, L., Mears, G., Vincent, W., & Hawes, S. (2011). The supervisory relationship when women supervise women: An exploratory study of power, reflexivity, collaboration, and authenticity. *The Clinical Supervisor, 30*(2), 141–171.

McDowell, T. (2004). Exploring the racial experience of therapists in training: A critical race theory perspective. *The American Journal of Family Therapy, 32*(4), 305–324.

McDowell, T., Brown, A. L., Cullen, N., & Duyn, A. (2013). Social class in family therapy education: Experiences of low SES students. *Journal of Marital and Family Therapy, 39*(1), 72–86.

Mittal, M., & Wieling, E. (2006). Training experiences of international doctoral students in marriage and family therapy. *Journal of Marital and Family Therapy, 32*(3), 369–383.

Piercy, F. P., Earl, R. M., Aldrich, R. K., Nguyen, H. N., Steelman, S. M., Haugen, E., ... Gary, E. (2016). Most and least meaningful learning experiences in marriage and family therapy education. *Journal of Marital and Family Therapy, 42*(4), 584–598.

Prouty, A. M., Helmeke, K. B., & Fischer, J. (2016). Mentorship in family therapy training programs: Students' and new graduates' perspectives. *Journal of Family Psychotherapy, 27*(1), 35–56.

Rastogi, M., & Wieling, E. (Eds.). (2005). *Voices of color: First-person accounts of ethnic minority therapists.* Thousand Oaks, CA: Sage

Meaningful and Fulfilling Training Experiences 4

The purpose of this chapter is to provide you with examples of existing ideas, models, and frameworks for meaningful and fulfilling training and supervision experiences on your journey to becoming an MFT. One of our goals is to empower you with information about good practices in our field related to MFT education, training, and supervision. Another goal is to encourage you to use this knowledge here to become empowered if you are not having a meaningful or fulfilling educational or supervision experience. We want you to know what kind of experiences are available to you and what researchers have found to support and facilitate personal and professional growth for students and supervisees.

We have organized this chapter in a way to inform you about the expectations you can have for your multiculturally informed education and training by reviewing the MFT educational standards. We then provide you with literature that demonstrates the positive ways MFT programs contribute to wholistic and fulfilling educational experiences, particularly on topics related to culture and diversity. We then follow that with literature regarding what supervisors are doing or can do to facilitate positive and culturally responsive supervision practices for both the supervisor and supervisee. Safe and practical steps will be thoughtfully presented so that supervisees can consider what a sense of empowerment in supervision might look and feel like during your development from student and trainee to postgraduate pre-licensed therapist.

Multicultural Training and Education Standards

Training experiences can occur in the classroom, in consultation with peers and colleagues, and in supervision. Training can be formal or informal. Typically on your journey to becoming a licensed MFT, the experiences you will have with training are more formalized. According to our national accrediting body, the Commission on Accreditation for Marriage and Family Therapy Education (COAMFTE), the following principles should guide education and training:

> A commitment to multiculturally-informed education that includes an understanding of how larger social processes lead to systemic inequality and disadvantage for diverse, marginalized, and/or underserved communities; and the responsibility of MFTs in addressing and intervening in these systems when working with systemically disadvantaged diverse, marginalized, and/or underserved communities.
>
> (p. 5)

> A commitment to an inclusive and diverse learning environment that considers student input, includes transparent processes and policies, and provides educational opportunities for a broad spectrum of students. This includes a commitment to treating all students with respect, equity, and appreciation regardless of their race, age, gender, ethnicity, sexual orientation, gender identity, socioeconomic status, disability, health status, religious and spiritual practices, nation of origin or other relevant social categories, immigration status, and language.
>
> (pp. 5–6)

In addition to the principles above, Standard II of the COAMFTE is a specific commitment to diversity and inclusion. This means that students who are training to become MFTs will be exposed to education that is considered to be grounded in and informed by multiculturally relevant content. For the MFT student, in the classroom, they should see the graduate program's commitment to diversity and inclusion in their learning outcomes and woven into all or most of their course content. In addition, the student should have a solid understanding of their graduate program's definition of what "diversity" means. Students should be able to identify what they have learned regarding topics such as race and ethnicity, gender, age, religion, sexual orientation, ability, etc. The graduate program climate should foster for all students, a sense of "safety, respect, and appreciation" (COAMFTE, 2014, p. 17). How this looks and feels will vary, of course, for students in the program, depending on their own intersecting identities as well as those of the other students and faculty. The standards also indicate that MFT students should gain direct experience, through course activities, clinical training, or in research, with "diverse, marginalized, and/or underserved communities" or "members of these communities" (p. 17).

In her years of research on the integration of multiculturalism into the field of MFT, McDowell (2004) has found that students are looking for much more than a program that says they value diversity but rather seek a program that demonstrates a commitment to diversity. A commitment to diversity might be demonstrated in the following ways: "a racially sensitive and collaborative atmosphere; critical consideration of race and white privilege; and the integration of multiple perspectives throughout coursework and supervision" (McDowell, 2004, p. 317). Students have indicated that a program truly committed to the integration of diversity creates space for dialogues about multiculturalism and equity in all courses and supervision. And during these dialogues students and faculty connect, respect, try to understand, and ultimately learn from each other (McDowell, 2004). Students are also looking for "diverse voices" to be represented in their curriculum—meaning the program or faculty intentionally integrate unique cultural experiences and perspectives into their courses, readings, and discussions across classes and when working on clinical cases, and in supervision.

A graduate program's commitment to and execution of these principles and standards will vary based on many factors. One of the goals of this chapter is to help you understand the ways that programs, instructors, and supervisors are successful. And when they are not successful, the ways you may help initiate or facilitate these practices on your own or with other like-minded colleagues in your own program or supervision.

Meaningful Multicultural Experiences in MFT Programs

Oftentimes, in MFT graduate programs, there is a single diversity course. The standard curriculum for such courses typically covers the topics of race, ethnicity, and gender. Some courses go beyond those topics and also include in depth exploration of the intersections of sexual orientation, age, class, socioeconomic status (SES), religion, ability, etc. and/or power, privilege, and oppression with clinical work.

Winston and Piercy (2010) completed a research study to understand how COAMFTE graduate programs are teaching about gender and diversity. Course syllabi were analyzed from 21 master's programs and 18 doctoral programs across the United States to understand to what extent the content related to diversity, power and privilege, age, culture, ethnicity, gender, ability, nationality, race, religion, sexual orientation, spirituality, and SES was covered. During the second phase of the study, Winston interviewed instructors from those programs about their experiences teaching those topics. What the researchers found was a revelation of the complexities inherent in teaching diversity courses. Specifically, the instructors shared that learning about topics in diversity is a lifelong process and in order to dig into the complex topics with students, it requires personal investment, reflection, and self-work on the part of the instructor *and* the student. When these courses are most successful is when the instructor models the challenging personal process through some personal sharing while also holding space for students to do the same (Winston & Piercy, 2010).

McDowell and Shelton (2002) discussed this same idea as the professor "positioning" themselves in the classroom, specifically telling students about themselves, what they believe in, and what is expected of students. This is not something that instructors necessarily learn how to do beforehand, and with each class and group of students, the dynamics change. It is important for the student in these spaces, where learning about the complexities of human diversity is the focus, to recognize their part in producing a worthwhile and intimate experience for themselves and their colleagues. While ultimately it is up to our instructors to begin these processes, it is students who must take risks and share their personal stories and who must contribute to the "safe" classroom environment by remaining open to the stories of others (Esmiol, Knudson-Martin, & Delgado, 2012). Instructors and supervisors may be needed to initiate, but it is students who must take action to bring their whole selves into the training and supervision and ultimately into the therapy room.

Most courses on the topics of diversity offer other vehicles for student engagement that may include a series of self-reflection assignments and outside of class experiences. Winston and Piercy (2010) found across many COAMFTE programs assignments such as classroom dialogue, journaling, community immersion experiences, and interviewing members of different cultural groups to help students increase their awareness and curiosity about others. Another purpose of such assignments and discussions was to help students become more personally connected to or invested in the subject matter. The hypothesis is that when students relate to the material they are leaning, they may become more sensitive to the various experiences of people and therefore enhance their clinical abilities in serving diverse populations (Winston & Piercy, 2010). The first step in having meaningful and fulfilling growth experiences related to these topics is to engage in our own critical self-reflection.

Critical Self-Reflection

Hardy and Laszloffy (1998) stated it best when they said:

> Because we believe the line between therapy and everyday life is blurred, we find it impossible for therapists to separate who they are outside therapy from who they are inside therapy ... Thus, the process of becoming racially [culturally] sensitive begins with how each therapist lives his or her life.
>
> (p. 125)

An important step in developing critical self-awareness begins with enhancing cultural or racial sensitivity. The process for becoming racially sensitive is lifelong. For people of color, the fact that "race matters" is nothing new. But for many White people, acknowledging and understanding that most of our social structures in society are centered in race can be difficult. This same discussion can be had for issues related to gender, sexual orientation, religion, and other topics. When people make the choice to be culturally and racially sensitive it means acknowledging that racism and other "isms" such as sexism, heterosexism, classism, and xenophobia are social structures that exist and influence every aspect of each of our lived experiences. Critical self-reflection is an invitation to examine the ways in which the "isms" impact your life and the lives of those around you *and* to acknowledge the ways in which you may contribute, often unintentionally, to maintaining these detrimental social structures.

In graduate programs, the first step of developing critical self-awareness is by the student engaging in self-reflection and developing greater awareness of various aspects of their own identity and cultural background. Previously, the primary focus of diversity education had been on issues of gender and race and ethnicity. Over time, however, developing greater racial and gender self-awareness has expanded in recognition of the multiple intersecting aspects of our identities. Intersectionality, discussed earlier in this book, takes into consideration the multiple aspects of our identity existing at once: gender, race and ethnicity, sexual orientation, class, religion, SES, ability, class, generation, etc. In more recent years, an additional emphasis has been placed on students examining their own experiences of power, privilege, and oppression as well (McDowell, 2004). In Chapter 6, we will provide you with several exercises that you may use on your own or in conjunction with a course in your MFT program, to help on your own journey of critical self-exploration and development. These exercises will be relevant no matter who you are or how you identify.

Classroom Engagement and Dialogue

A primary vehicle for many students for learning about power, privilege, and oppression is typically via classroom engagement and dialogue. McDowell and Shelton (2002) discuss the complexities of managing difficult dialogues with students related to these topics as do other writers (Esmiol, Knudson-Martin, & Delgado, 2012; Patrick & Connolly, 2013). For some students in MFT programs, it is the first time they have been exposed to concepts of power and privilege and for others, these topics may be at the center of their life and reflective of their everyday lived experiences. When students are invited to express their thoughts, feelings, and beliefs and they are encouraged "to question, evaluate, and discuss the ideas" such as privilege, oppression, and racism, in light of their own experiences, dilemmas may arise (McDowell & Shelton, 2002, p. 317). For example, some students may feel marginalized by others in the classroom or some students may express a view that does not match that of the professor or other students resulting in their own anger or defensiveness (Patrick & Connolly, 2013). Such conversations, even when facilitated well, can leave students (and the instructor) feeling defensive. In these situations, it is up to the professor (sometimes with the help of students) to find ways to push the students beyond their feelings of marginalization and potential shutdown, to a place of grappling, processing, and evolving.

Journaling

Journaling is an opportunity for students to reflect on what they are learning in their program and to explore how new ideas and concepts may be congruent with or in conflict with their own assumptions (McDowell & Shelton, 2002). Journals offer students a place to work through assumptions and challenges related to course content and classroom dynamics. In addition, journals also help instructors to get a clearer understanding of what students may be challenged by when topics related to diversity come up in readings, classroom and case discussions, and course assignments. In their research study, focused on critical incidents for 19 MFT doctoral students, Lee and Vennum (2010) found that student journaling about "cultural bumps" facilitated reflection and raising of their own consciousness about perceptions, beliefs, feelings, and actions. Cultural bumps are understood as times or incidents in which the individual's awareness about the influence of their own culture on the ways in which they think and behave are logged into journals and reflected on by participants. Critical incident journaling was initially used to help MFT educators and supervisors to become more self-aware of their own beliefs and biases about diversity factors. Then those educators and supervisors could use the same method of increasing self-awareness that they had learned with their own students and supervisees. Critical incident journaling is an active and personal process, and because of this, the learning that takes place may be experienced as more credible for the individual (Lee & Vennum, 2010). The outcomes when individuals engage in critical incident journaling can increase multicultural curiosity and awareness as well as pursuit of more opportunities to learn about themselves and those who are different.

Immersion Experiences

Experiential learning can be a large part of the education of future MFTs. This can include experiences such as role-plays, participating in interventions, personal therapy, or immersion experiences. Specifically, experiential learning related to promoting increased awareness and understanding of diversity involves "cultural plunges" (Laszloffy & Habekost, 2010) into an environment that is unfamiliar to the student. Examples of these experiences might be visiting a church of a different religion or in a monolithic community; participating in a cultural ceremony; taking part in a protest or march; or interviewing someone who has differing identities. Instructors have found that these types of experiences "enhance cultural sensitivity" for their students (Laszloffy & Habekost, 2010). Cultural sensitivity is defined as "a state of attunement to, emotional resonance with, and meaningful responsiveness to the needs and feelings of others" (Laszloffy & Habekost, 2010, p. 334). Through immersive experiential learning tasks in the real world, students have the opportunity to actively engage in relating to others across differences and to put themselves in the position of being the minority. The result of directly interacting with or being in the subjugated position encourages students to begin the process of moving beyond awareness to developing sensitivity regarding the unique and diverse experiences of others.

Mentorship and Support

Mentorship in the profession of MFT is not formalized, but reported by supervisees as an influential aspect of their growth and development (Hernández, Taylor, & McDowell, 2009; Kelly & Boyd-Franklin, 2005). When mentorship is not formalized or accessible, particularly mentorship related to gender, being a person of color, or for people from other subjugated groups, there is a burden for those who share subjugated social locations to find mentors outside of the profession (but within their own cultural group), or to create their own pathway for mentorship and support with peers, or to become the mentors themselves as they move into licensed and faculty positions in the field.

An example of a meaningful training experience was in the creation of a mentor-support group for therapists of color (Watts-Jones et al., 2007). Therapists of color, women, and other minority groups report the need for "support and validation, in their clinical training experiences" to process "experiences of estrangement, invisibility, and devaluation" as well as racism as a trainee (p. 443). The creation of a space, in which therapists-of-color in training were provided a group environment with faculty-of-color mentors, for support and feedback regarding their clinical training and personal process and to discuss clinical work with clients of color away from "White eyes" proved powerful for those involved. Topics explored included the therapists' personal experiences of racism and/or observations of oppressive behaviors and actions at their training clinics or in their program. The group also explored intergroup tensions among themselves as a diverse group of therapists-of-color (Watts-Jones et al., 2007). Such groups may take the form of student-led process groups or faculty-led mentoring groups. Other possible formats might include a group facilitated by someone connected to the field but outside the graduate program or training site.

One of the goals of all of this work is for you, the student, to translate what you are learning in the classroom and in trainings into your own life and into your work as therapists (Esmiol, Knudson-Martin, & Delgado, 2012). What you, the student, can take away from such research studies is the importance of investing yourselves into the process of learning. These courses and associated learning experiences require personal investment and stretching, often beyond your comfort zone. It is when the students and instructors work together that this is most successful.

Meaningful and Fulfilling Supervision Experiences

Clinical supervision is required for students of marriage and family therapy during graduate school while seeing clients in the field as a trainee and post-graduation while seeing clients and accruing hours toward licensure. Pre-licensed, post-master's degree therapists are referred to differently in various states; examples include registered intern or clinical associate. For the purposes of this section, we will use the term supervisee, referring to both trainees and post-graduate, pre-licensed clinicians. The purpose of clinical supervision is to provide the supervisee guidance and support with their clinical cases and to facilitate self-of-the-therapist development (AAMFT, 2014). Further, the supervisor is charged with helping the supervisee develop competence as a marriage and family therapist in the areas of empathy, theory, techniques, and cultural sensitivity (Rigazio-DiGilio, 2016). The supervisor evaluates the supervisee's skills and works with the supervisee to develop the competencies necessary to be an effective therapist. It is clinical supervisors who serve as "gatekeepers for the profession" of marriage and family therapy (Rigazio-DiGilio, 2016, p. 25) and determine a supervisee's eventual readiness for licensure.

In relation to supervision, some common questions for beginning therapists are: What makes a good supervisor? How will I know a supervisor's approach in supervision? What kind of questions may I ask, to help build a positive and growth supporting supervision environment? How will I bring my whole self, including various aspects of my intersecting identities and values into the supervision relationship? What constitutes multicultural or "culturally competent" supervision?

According to the *AAMFT Approved Supervision Designation Handbook*, supervisors provide trainees and interns in marriage and family therapy oversight, training, and evaluation for the supervisee's development of clinical skills using relational or systemic approaches (AAMFT, 2014).

Supervisors of MFTs should demonstrate the following in their supervision practices with their trainees and interns: evidence of systemic thinking; clarity of purpose and goals for the supervision process; clarity of supervisory roles and relationships; preferred supervision model or practices; evidence of sensitivity and attention to contextual factors such as developmental phase of the trainee, culture, race, ethnicity, sexual orientation, age, sex, gender, economics, power, and privilege; and evidence of sensitivity to and competency in ethics and legal factors of supervision (AAMFT, 2014, p. 22). In addition, supervisors are expected to remain current about recent developments in the field of MFT; about new and useful approaches to supervision; about best practices for screening, assessing, and evaluating supervisees; with integrating and managing cultural factors into supervision; about ethical and legal considerations for therapy and supervision; and about supervising challenging situations, mentoring processes, and troubleshooting (AAMFT, 2014, pp. 23–24). When supervisors make clear their adherence to and valuing of the Approved Supervisor standards, the supervisee may rest assured they have a solid beginning foundation for a meaningful and fulfilling supervision experience.

Your Supervisor(s) and Supervision Relationship(s)

One of the most important relationships you will have as a developing therapist is the one with your supervisor (and for most of you it will likely be multiple supervisors on your road to licensure). Not all supervision relationships will be superb, not all will be close; but the hope is that most of them will facilitate your growth and development as a person and as a therapist. Nelson and colleagues (2008) described the complexity of the supervision relationship as interpersonal in that it is designed to both help the supervisee to grow personally and develop as a clinician. Additionally, supervising, educating, and training therapists is all with the intention that you, the supervisee, will become a future colleague. The onus of responsibility for the supervisor is to help the therapist-in-training to become competent and confident and eventually an equal in the field (Falender, 2010). To add to the complexity of these dynamics, it is supervisors who are ultimately responsible for client welfare simultaneous with clinician development and it is supervisors who must balance support and feedback to help you facilitate productive therapy and to undergo your own growth. Each level of the relationships the supervisor is managing, supervisor–supervisee and trainee–client, are all couched in socio-political, sociocultural contexts, and realities.

A good supervision relationship starts by establishing a foundation of safety for the supervision alliance that will facilitate the mutual growth of trust between the supervisor and supervisee (Nelson et al., 2008). Researchers have found that the strongest supervision alliances occur in environments that are open, respectful, and supportive (Anderson, Schlossberg, & Rigazio-DiGilio, 2000). Supervisees experience supervision more positively when they perceive their supervisor as both trustworthy with the supervisee's vulnerabilities and as possessing expertise to guide their clinical work as therapists. This means that when a supervisor is able to facilitate a balance between the therapist's personal growth and the development of their clinical skills, you as a trainee will be more satisfied (Anderson, Schlossberg, & Rigazio-DiGilio, 2000).

Rigazio-DiGilio (2016) explains that establishing a solid and safe foundation for supervision requires "supervisory exchanges that promote educational clarity, specificity, and shared understandings that emphasize mutual sharing" between the supervisor and supervisee from the start of the supervision relationship (p. 29). This means that the supervisor will share or disclose personally, when appropriate, to build rapport and encourage supervisee self-disclosures. In addition, it is also critical for the supervisor to acknowledge educational and training gaps between them and their supervisees. There will be times when you, the supervisee, are more current and up to date or have relevant personal experiences, and the supervisors who acknowledge this and use your expertise will benefit all involved in the supervision.

To simplify our overview of what we believe to be factors that contribute to strong supervision relationships, the following outline summarizes what we have found in the literature to be important factors for the supervisor to actively consider and incorporate in their work with you, the supervisee (Falender & Shrfranske, 2012; Mangione, Mears, Vincent, & Hawes, 2011).

1. Safety

    a. Acknowledging hierarchy
    b. Acknowledging power differentials
    c. Discussing demographic differences between supervisor and supervisee
    d. Being transparent about evaluative process and functions of supervision
    e. Ongoing opportunities for feedback, reflection, and discussion about supervision and supervision relationship

2. Clear expectations from the beginning (supervision contracts)

   a. Outlining the supervisor's responsibility
   b. Outlining the supervisee's responsibility
   c. Learning objectives
   d. Structure of supervision
   e. Evaluation criteria

3. Respect, authenticity/congruence, and genuine curiosity

   a. Valuing what each member of the supervision system has to contribute
   b. Using self-disclosure meaningfully and appropriately
   c. Exploring the supervisee's perspectives, motives, and rationale
   d. Direct communication; both supportive and challenging

4. Consideration of supervisor's and supervisee's intersecting identities, cultural values, and influence on supervision, therapist development, and clients

   a. Discussing identity, cultural values, and issues within the supervision relationship
   b. Discussing identity, cultural values and issues as they relate to the supervisee and their clients
   c. Discussing identity, cultural values and issues as they intersect with professional development

Multicultural and Feminist Informed Supervision

When considering bringing your whole self into supervision and your work as a therapist, there are supervision philosophies that invite you to do so from the start. Researchers report that multicultural and feminist-informed supervision practices have a foundation that integrates intentional examination of human diversity and power dynamics at the levels of self-of-the-supervisor and self-of-the-therapist and within the supervision relationship as well (Prouty & Twist, 2016). Green and Dekkers (2010) explain that when supervisors attend to power and diversity in supervision, it contributes to learning outcomes and overall supervisee satisfaction with supervision.

Multicultural Supervision

Multicultural supervision is often cited as supervision between a supervisor and supervisee who are ethnically or racially different (Dressel et al., 2007). However, we believe that multicultural supervision involves several more elements. For our purposes, when we refer to multicultural supervision, we mean supervision that attends to diversity by integrating issues of culture, intersecting identities (e.g. age, race, ethnicity, gender, sexual orientation, religion, social class, ability, etc.), power, privilege, oppression, and social justice into various aspects of supervision.

Multicultural supervision integrates interpersonal discussions about the culture and identity of the supervisor and supervisee to openly explore how each might impact the supervision relationship. The supervisor creates space for discussions about identity and culture as it relates to the therapist and client relationship. And finally, cultural sensitivity and awareness is integrated into the entire supervision experience, not just when varying identities and culture are apparent (for the supervisor, supervisee, or client), but overall acknowledging that identity and culture are important to consider throughout all aspects of supervision. Supervision that is culturally pertinent involves supervisors helping therapists to increase their cultural awareness, to evaluate the cultural relevance of theory and treatment models, and to examine the impact of culture on and within the supervisory relationship (Ancis & Marshall, 2010). For the purposes of developing your whole self as a clinician, we believe thinking of multicultural supervision in these terms will be most beneficial to you as a supervisee.

Feminist Informed Supervision

Feminist informed supervision includes a social justice perspective and works to eliminate oppressive interactions in the supervisory relationship (Green & Dekkers, 2010). This means that the supervisor uses respect and encourages a reciprocal relationship with her supervisee that includes mutually beneficial self-disclosure, both supervisor and supervisee asking questions, and dealing directly with conflict. Feminist supervision is considered collaborative, empowering, and strengths-based (Degges-White, Colon, & Borzumato-Gainy, 2013). A critical component of this process involves open acknowledgement and direct discussions about power and hierarchy in an effort to encourage the supervisee to use their voice to express ideas and opinions about their own clinical work, growth, and development. "Open discussion of power means: using the term power when discussing it, talking about power at the first supervision session, and revisiting power as a discussion topic throughout the supervisory relationship" (Murphy & Wright, 2005, p. 293).

What Supervisees Want

Our review of the literature shows that supervisees actually want supervisors who are actively engaged in the processes reviewed above. This is particularly true for supervisees who have marginalized or subjugated parts of their identities. When the supervisor creates an open and "safe" climate in supervision for intentional discussions about diversity, supervisees report a "strong working alliance" (Ancis & Marshall, 2010, p. 283). Supervision is considered culturally relevant when supervisors are aware of and facilitate discussions about the impact of the supervisor's, the supervisee's, and the client's culture on the supervision process. Supervisees express the significance of having a supervisor with critical consciousness as important to their development as therapists and their work with their clients, particularly clients of color (Hernández, Taylor, & McDowell, 2009).

Specifically, discussing race in supervision is an important part of developing a professional identity for the supervisee, as it invites the supervisee to bring aspects of their personal identity into their professional identity (Cook, 1994). A supervisor who facilitates discussions about race, including the race of the supervisee, the supervisor, and the client helps to foster "authentic therapy and supervisory" relationships. When supervisors discuss race in supervision, in spite of their possible discomfort, they model for their supervisees how race may be talked about in therapy with their clients. Overwhelmingly, students report that what is most helpful for them, as they navigate instances of racism in the therapy room from their clients, is to have open discussions about that experience in supervision (Ali et al., 2005).

The Challenges of Getting There

As was discussed in Chapter 4, and one problem consistently noted in the literature, regarding training and supervision, is the lack of initiative on the instructor's or supervisor's part to discuss racism, oppression, power and privilege, and social location with students and supervisees (Garcia et al., 2009; Hernández, Taylor, & McDowell, 2009). When students and supervisees feel silenced and oppressed by racism and other *isms*, it may affect both their personal and clinical self-confidence and development (Ali et al., 2005). So the questions that may come up as you navigate this journey include: What if my supervisor does not bring these things up? How do I bring it up first? How can I determine safety for this type of engagement in my education and training? These important questions will be addressed in Chapter 7 when we offer you a model for engagement with various people on your journey becoming an MFT, including professors and supervisors. Ultimately, we hope this chapter has given you insight and hope for many of the meaningful and fulfilling experiences you will have in your educational and clinical training settings on this journey.

Summary

This chapter highlights the literature regarding what you should expect from your educational experience in your MFT graduate program in terms of integration of multicultural perspectives across the curriculum. Many programs and faculty have made great strides utilizing classroom discussions, readings, and reflective and immersive experiences. When faculty and students are regularly engaged in critical discussions and reflection, all benefit. Supervision that supports the growth and development as well as the likelihood that the therapist will bring their whole selves into their work involves a supervisor who is critically conscious, collaborative, and invites the various aspects of the supervisee's contributions to clinical work. When supervisors invite discussions about race, gender, and other aspects of social location (as it relates to the supervisor, supervisee, and the clients) into the supervision discussion, supervisees experience more growth and satisfaction in their clinical development. We hope this chapter enables you to mark the aspects of your education and training that have been meaningful and helps you to find ways you can ask for more of what you need to enhance your journey.

Questions for Reflection

1. In what ways does/did your MFT program integrate multicultural education standards into the curriculum?
2. How are/were you encouraged to engage in critical self-reflection and dialogue regarding your social location and that of others? In what ways do/did your faculty demonstrate their own ongoing engagement in critical self-reflection?
3. What kind of mentorship is/was available to you in your graduate program? At your field site? How has mentorship served you on your journey to becoming an MFT?

4. In what ways has your supervision facilitated you using your voice, integrating your social location, and bringing your whole self into your work as a therapist?
5. In what ways do the conceptual frameworks of multicultural and/or feminist-informed supervision match your needs as supervisee? How does your current supervisor utilize concepts from these frameworks in their work with you?

References

AAMFT (2014). *Approved supervision designation: Standards handbook (effective January 2014 version 4)*. Retrieved from http://dx5br1z4f6n0k.cloudfront.net/imis15/Documents/Supervision/2017%20S pervision/June%202015_AS%20Handbook%20ver_Oct_%202016_toc%20to%20b %20edited.pdf

Ali, S. R., Flojo, J. R., Chronister, K. M., Hayashino, D., Smiling, Q. R., Torres, D., & McWhirter, E. H. (2005). When racism is reversed: Therapists of color speak about their experiences with racism from clients, supervisees, and supervisors. In M. Rastogi & E. Wieling (Eds.), *Voices of color: First-person accounts of ethnic minority therapists* (pp. 117–133). Thousand Oaks, CA: Sage.

Ancis, J. R., & Marshall, D. S. (2010). Using a multicultural framework to assess supervisees' perceptions of culturally competent supervision. *Journal of Counseling and Development, 88*(3), 277–284.

Anderson, S. A., Schlossberg, M., & Rigazio-DiGilio, S. (2000). Family therapy trainees' evaluations of their best and worst supervision experiences. *Journal of Marital and Family Therapy, 26*(1), 79–91.

Commission on Accreditation for Marriage and Family Therapy Education (2014). *Accreditation standards: Graduate & post-graduate marriage and family therapy training programs* Version 12.0. Alexandria, VA: Author.

Cook, D. A. (1994). Racial identity in supervision. *Counselor Education & Supervision, 34*(2), 132–141.

Degges-White, S. E., Colon, B. R., & Borzumato-Gainy, C. (2013). Counseling supervision within a feminist framework: Guidelines for intervention. *Journal of Humanistic Counseling, 52*, 92–105.

Dressel, J. L., Consoli, A. J., Kim, B. S. K., & Atkinson, D. R. (2007). Successful and unsuccessful multicultural supervisory behaviors: A Delphi poll. *Journal of Multicultural Counseling and Development, 35*, 51–64.

Esmiol, E. E., Knudson-Martin, C., & Delgado, S. (2012). Developing a contextual consciousness: Learning to address gender, societal power, and culture in clinical practice. *Journal of Marital and Family Therapy, 38*(4), 573–588.

Falender, C. A. (2010). Relationship and accountability: Tensions in feminist supervision. *Women & Therapy, 33*, 22–41.

Falender, C. A., & Shrfranske, E. P. (2012). *Getting the most out of clinical training and supervision: A guide for practicum students and interns*. Washington, DC: American Psychological Association.

Garcia, M., Kosutic, I., McDowell, T., & Anderson, S. A. (2009). Raising critical consciousness in family therapy supervision. *Journal of Feminist Family Therapy, 21*, 18–38.

Green, M. S., & Dekkers, T. D. (2010). Attending to power and diversity in supervision: An exploration of supervisee learning outcomes and satisfaction with supervision. *Journal of Feminist Family Therapy, 22*, 293–312. doi:10.1080/08952833.2010.528703

Hardy, K. V., & Laszloffy, T. A. (1998). The dynamics of a pro-racist ideology: Implications for family therapists. In M. McGoldrick (Ed.), *Re-visioning family therapy: Race, culture, and gender in clinical practice* (pp. 118–128). New York: Guilford.

Hernández, P., Taylor, B. A., & McDowell, T. (2009). Listening to ethnic minority AAMFT approved supervisors' reflections on their experiences as supervisees. *Journal of Systemic Therapies, 28*(1), 88–100.

Kelly, S., & Boyd-Franklin, N. (2005). African American women in client, therapist, and supervisory relationships: The parallel processes of race, culture, and family. In M. Rastogi & E. Wieling (Eds.), *Voices of color: First-person accounts of ethnic minority therapists* (pp. 67–89). Thousand Oaks, CA: Sage.

Laszloffy, T., & Habekost, J. (2010). Using experiential tasks to enhance cultural sensitivity among MFT trainees. *Journal of Marital and Family Therapy, 36*(3), 333–346.

Lee, M. M., & Vennum, A. V. (2010). Using critical incident journaling to encourage cultural awareness in doctoral marriage and family therapy students. *Journal of Family Psychotherapy, 21*, 238–252.

Mangione, L., Mears, G., Vincent, W., & Hawes, S. (2011). The supervisory relationship when women supervise women: An exploratory study of power, reflexivity, collaboration and authenticity. *The Clinical Supervisor, 30*, 141–171. DOI: 10.1080/07325223.2011.604272

McDowell, T. (2004). Exploring the racial experience of therapists in training: A critical race theory perspective. *The American Journal of Family Therapy, 32*(4), 305–324.

McDowell, T., & Shelton, D. (2002). Valuing ideas of social justice in MFT curricula. *Contemporary Family Therapy, 24*(2), 313–331.

Murphy, M. J., & Wright, D. W. (2005). Supervisees' perspectives of power use in supervision. *Journal of Marital and Family Therapy, 31*(3), 283–295.

Nelson, M. L., Barnes, K. L., Evans, A. L., & Triggiano, P. J. (2008). Working with conflict in clinical supervision: Wise supervisors' perspectives. *Journal of Counseling Psychology, 55*(2), 172–184.

Patrick, S., & Connolly, C. M. (2013). The privilege project: A narrative approach for teaching social justice and multicultural awareness. *Journal of Systemic Therapies, 32*(1), 70–86.

Prouty, A. M., & Twist, M. L. C. (2016). Training feminist family therapists. In K. Jordan (Ed.), *Couple, marriage, and family therapy supervision* (pp. 347–367). New York: Springer.

Rigazio-DiGilio, S. A. (2016). MFT supervision: An overview. In K. Jordan (Ed.), *Couple, marriage, and family therapy supervision* (pp. 25–49). New York: Springer.

Watts-Jones, D., Ali, R., Alfaro, J., & Frederick, A. (2007). The role of a mentoring group for family therapy trainees and therapists of color. *Family Process, 46*, 437–450.

Winston, E. J., & Piercy, F. P. (2010). Gender and diversity topics taught in commission on accreditation for marriage and family therapy education programs. *Journal of Marital and Family Therapy, 36*(4), 446–471.

Students' and Supervisees' Stories

5

At the time of writing this book, we have been teaching and supervising for 22 years (collectively). Because of the contexts in which we have been teaching and supervising, the majority of our students and trainees identify with having at least one or more intersecting marginalized identities. It is because of their stories, their trust in us, and our shared growth that we envisioned this book.

As our students and trainees shared with us their experiences of microaggressions, overt *-isms* or expressed sentiments of inadequacy, we were reminded of our own training experiences. We realized how common it is for students and those early in their MFT training to face challenging situations shaped by their clinical or academic experiences. If beginning MFTs and supervisors/professors could hear and listen to these stories, perhaps those with marginalized identities might be encouraged to persist in the field. We also wanted to highlight the stories of empowerment and support because there are many. These shape a student/trainee's identity for years to come.

We believe that stories and lived experience—knowing our own and encountering that of others—are foundational to growth and transformation. In addition to research literature and theoretical propositions, we want to ground this book in the narratives of our students, former students/trainees, and dear colleagues.

How We Sought Stories

In planning for this chapter, we reflected upon the students and colleagues we have met and had the opportunity to work with over the years and the ways their stories and experiences have shaped us. We are grateful for the wealth of diversity in our supervisory and teaching experiences. Consequently, we could reach out to students and colleagues with identities reflecting different social locations to see if they had interest in submitting their stories for consideration for this book. Here is the text of the email we initially sent out:

> We are delighted to be working on a manuscript for a book titled *Finding Voice and Flourishing as Beginning MFTs*. The purpose of the book is to highlight MFTs in training with diverse experiences to empower future therapists in training so that they may feel seen and encouraged to grow into more authentic therapists. In this book we will include stories from current and past students, supervisees, and colleagues. We believe you have a powerful story and would like to invite you to submit a contribution for possible inclusion in this book. I thought of you because I value your perspective, consciousness, and experience as a person with intersectional identities and rich life experiences. I am thinking in particular about your understanding of [particular experience/identity]. We are aware that such stories can be difficult to share publicly, so your identity can be anonymous or shared.
>
> We are looking for concrete examples of both challenges and meaningful experiences involving the social location of the trainee in supervision relationships, with clients, with therapist colleagues, and in the classroom. These may include experiences of disempowerment, microaggressions, and dissatisfaction or experiences of support, safety, and connection.

The majority of those we emailed responded in excitement and were enthused to submit their contributions. A few never responded and a few others did not have time in this particular season of life. The two of us read through their submissions and considered what sort of feedback would be helpful to offer and what edit requests would allow for readers to better grasp their stories. After a few email exchanges and mutually agreed upon edits, these are their stories that we are excited to share.

The Stories

Each contributor, appearing in alphabetical order by first name, will briefly introduce themselves and their context and stories will follow. You will see their biographies highlighted in the boxes with a section for "keywords." These are glossary terms (Chapter 1) and/or social location identifiers (please see Chapter 6 and the ADDRESSING framework) present in their narratives. If the contributor chose to respond to more than one question (difficult supervision experiences, difficult training/student experiences, meaningful experiences), we have delineated those with lines. At the end of each contribution we offer a brief reflection on the themes from each of their narratives.

> **Asha Sutton**
>
> Asha is 35 years old and identifies as a cisgender, heterosexual, U.S.-born, African American female. She is currently able-bodied and connected to middle to upper middle-class contexts. She grew up in the suburbs of Chicago, attending Hampton University (private university) for undergraduate studies and Michigan State University (public state university) for her master's and PhD in MFT. During her years as a trainee and intern, she worked at a university counseling clinic which served court-ordered clients involved in the child welfare and foster care system. All of her supervisors have been White men or women and the majority of her clients have been from lower to working-class communities. She currently teaches and provides clinical supervision for a COAMFTE-accredited master's and PhD program.
>
> **Keywords**: African American, female, race/ethnicity, gender, intersectionality

Clinical supervision is a unique process by which MFTs in training enter a sacred space which requires them to consume information as a scholar and demonstrate keen critical analysis skills, yet be open, vulnerable, and trusting of the unfolding supervision experience in order to identify possible triggers and reduce countertransference. I found consuming the space of a learner and scholar to be easiest. Whether reading a book, sitting through a lecture, or viewing clinical footage of the pioneers in the field, the information was there. All I had to do was consume and process the information and that always seemed to come easy to me.

The being open, vulnerable, and trusting of the process was a considerable challenge for me as a trainee. Two semesters left a particularly profound impact on my training experience. Working in a university counseling center setting, I worked with an older White male supervisor and another White male graduate student. It was just the three of us. The supervisor was quite influential in the program, as well as in the larger department. In overt and covert ways, this was made clear. The male student and I were approximately at the same place in our graduate training with regards to coursework and clinical hours.

During our weekly two-hour meetings, I often felt left out of the conversation. The two males would banter back and forth and discuss random topics that I had little interest in (e.g. fishing, growing up in the South, hiking, etc.). I recall thinking to myself, "Do they even realize that there is someone else in the room?" I often found myself randomly nodding my head and smiling all while hoping that my facial expressions showed that I had some remote interest in the mundane topics.

It was in these moments that my intersectionality felt particularly conflicted. I have strongly identified as a Black woman but through my training, my professional identity as an MFT was emerging. The developing MFT in me said, "Be open and vulnerable so that you can gain the most out of this essential component of your training. It's necessary to help you grow." My identity as a Black woman told me to "play the game." For me that meant finding balance between being approachable yet subtly letting others know my serious nature to ensure my success. It meant being strategic in my interactions to the extent that I couldn't burn bridges because despite my negative perceptions of my supervisor, I did in fact need him to sign off on my clinical paperwork and I did not need any obstacles that would impede this goal. This required giving my supervisor just enough openness to appease him in my effort, yet not allowing myself to fully engage in the process out of fear that my vulnerability would be used against me.

I consciously made the decision to withhold thoughts, ideas, and experiences because in my head the professional benefit was not worth the personal risk. I was the first person in my family to pursue a doctorate. Simply put, I wasn't willing to risk all that

I had worked for, all my family had worked for. I had seen and heard from other colleagues of color that being trusting didn't always yield the desired results. I wasn't daring enough to risk it all.

In many ways, my dissertation committee chair helped me to develop my strength and capacity as a doctoral female student of color. Upon meeting other graduate students in my cohort, I found it a bit odd that my assigned mentor was outside of the marriage and family therapy program. She was a tenured Black professor who was well-respected within the department. Despite being outside of my program, I was thrilled to be working with her because during the interview process she was particularly welcoming towards me.

While it was known that my assigned mentor could be replaced for another chairperson of my choosing, I ultimately made the decision to name her the chair of my dissertation committee. There is much to be considered when identifying a committee chair. Identifying a faculty that has a common research interest is one consideration; however, I made the decision to align myself with a chair that would support me emotionally as well as challenge me intellectually. As a student of color, who often felt like an outsider, this was something that I knew I needed in order to be successful. Her intelligence was undeniable but coupling her intelligence with her genuine care and concern for students was a winning combination in my book.

Leading up to my dissertation work, my interactions with her showed me that I could trust her and that she had my best interest at heart. She became an integral member of my village. Both overtly and covertly, she rallied around me to ensure that I was protected against department and university politics. She believed in me and was an advocate for my success.

I will never forget a poignant conversation that occurred between my chair and me during the writing process of my dissertation. I was working to meet a deadline I had set for myself. She had provided me with some particularly difficult feedback regarding my work, which threatened my ability to meet my self-imposed deadline. In that moment, I felt safe enough to tell her that she was a "dream crusher." She laughed hysterically in disbelief of my comment and then responded, "I'm not crushing your dreams. I am trying to make the work better. I know you can do it." All of these things were absolutely true. In that moment, her feedback was difficult to digest. Yet at the end of the day, I trusted her and her intentions. We shared laughter in that moment and still to this day we laugh at our recollection of the exchange.

Yes, she was my committee chair but more importantly she was a critical member of my support community. Her intentions were consistently pure in that she wanted me to succeed. It was through my experience with her that she demonstrated how vitally important it is to support other women and men of color going through challenging experiences and underscore that you can accomplish this while still being your authentic self.

> **Themes**: Asha's critical consciousness made her aware of her intersectional identity and how she interacted within a supervisory context with two White men. In a strategic manner, she had to weigh the risks and benefits of authenticity and professionalism. She also had the meaningful experience of being mentored by a Black female professor who used her relational power to empower Asha.

Chris Abounayan

Chris is 30 years old and identifies as a cisgender, heterosexual, U.S.-born, spiritual but not religious, second-generation Armenian American male. He is currently able-bodied and connected to upper middle-class contexts. He grew up in the San Fernando Valley of Los Angeles. Chris attended a private Armenian school which was culturally and religiously influenced from pre-kindergarten until his senior year. Later he attended the University of California, Santa Barbara for his undergraduate studies and California State University, Northridge for his master's degree in MFT. During his years as a trainee and intern, he worked with clients from low socioeconomic backgrounds who had open cases with Department of Children and Family Services. Additionally, Chris worked with clients struggling with addiction from low to very high socioeconomic status from a diverse array of cultural backgrounds. The majority of his supervisors have been White females.

Keywords: Armenian, ethnicity, culture, language, second generation, self-of-the-therapist

I recall a time during my experience as a trainee which was very frustrating. I identify as a second-generation Armenian American. The dialect of Armenian that I speak is considered "Western" with Lebanese influences. The clients with whom I was working were a first-generation Armenian couple and spoke the "Eastern" dialect with Russian influences. I found myself feeling nervous for the first session. I was preoccupied with fears about communicating with my clients in a way that was clear and effective. My insecurities were focused on the fact that I was second generation and "white washed" compared to them. I was worried that they would judge me as an inferior Armenian because I did not understand particular customs or culturally appropriate social norms. I was relieved to see that after some time I felt more comfortable with them. In moments where I could not understand what my clients were saying I disclosed that fact and sought clarification. My clients were happy to oblige and asked the same from me. Over time we developed a sense of connection in sharing our versions of "Western" and "Eastern" Armenian-ness. I was grateful for this experience of connection, as I felt alone in my journey with these clients.

My supervisor was not Armenian and understood very little about the culture in general or the particular differences between my cultural identity and that of my clients. To make matters even more complex, the social worker assigned to the clients was changed multiple times. Of the three social workers the clients had been assigned only one was Armenian. The two non-Armenian social workers expected me to act as a therapist, as a client advocate, and as a translator. In a sense I felt as though I was a poorly equipped tour guide tasked with the responsibility of taking the social workers on an Armenian vacation while at the same time I, too, was also unfamiliar with the territory. Many of the issues the clients faced during their case stemmed from cultural differences and language barriers. I did the best that I could to help the clients grow while simultaneously meeting the social worker's goals. I felt a heavy burden when their case closed, due to news of the female client's pregnancy, because I knew it would reopen and possibly get extended. The guilt I experienced stemmed from feelings of leaving the clients in a foreign judicial and social services system without a translator. Though I felt I did my best in helping these clients I often found myself wondering "was I 'Armenian enough' to truly be effective with them?" Despite the support of my supervisor, this was a question I grappled with alone.

> **Themes**: Chris wrestled with being in the in-between space as a second-generation Armenian American—wanting to support his Armenian clients, but being pushed into the role of cultural expert and guide when he did not feel equipped to do so nor was it his role as the therapist. His supervisor did not have an understanding of the bicultural struggles of adult children of immigrants and how this can contribute to his sense of clinical stress and inadequacy. The social workers assumed sameness of people with an Armenian background, a common mistake that people make of other racial, ethnic, or cultural groups they know little about.

Yang

Yang is a 35-year-old heterosexual female who was born in Taiwan. Yang earned her bachelor's degree in counseling and worked in school systems for three years as a guidance counselor. She received both master and doctoral degrees from AAMFT-accredited programs. She worked in community agencies, a hospital, a local correctional facility, and non-profit organizations as an intern during her master's and doctoral program. The supervisors she worked with were Caucasian men and women. Yang currently works as a behavioral therapist in a local hospital in the Midwest.

Keywords: Taiwanese, culture, communication style, international student, language

When I first started my practicum (first summer semester in the master's program), I was nervous about being in group supervision because I was unable to process information so quickly. The majority of my cohort members were Caucasian Americans. I was the only one in the group that wasn't a native speaker. My supervisor asked people to feel free to "jump in" if they have something to contribute, which is a style I wasn't comfortable with.

I was quiet most of the time during practicum because I could not keep up with the speed. When I met with the supervisor for dyadic supervision, he pointed out that I wasn't participating much in group and he would like to hear from me more. I was terrified (because I didn't want to make a bad impression as we just started supervision) and tried to think about a good explanation for why I wasn't talking much in the group. In our next dyadic meeting, I explained to my supervisor that I wasn't talking because I was very self-conscious and worried that I would say something wrong in front of my cohort. I also mentioned that it took me longer to understand what people were saying, as I am an international student whose native language isn't English. My supervisor told me that I was being defensive and just "didn't want to take feedback." I tried to explain but somehow I made the situation worse. The supervisor told me that this will reflect on my grade for practicum as I didn't participate in the group discussion. After this meeting, I felt so overwhelmed thinking that I was going to fail the class and wouldn't be able to move on with the rest of the cohort. A few days later, I spoke with my advisor about this experience because I was too anxious about failing the class that I wasn't able to concentrate in other classes. After several different conversations with different faculty members, I was transferred to a different practicum group with a different supervisor.

During the first semester in my doctoral training, I didn't receive a full assistantship like the rest of my colleagues. I only received a half assistantship (10hr/week) as an intern therapist for a collaboration project in the community, which didn't qualify for any tuition-waiver. This was particularly challenging due to my status as an international student (being on an F-1 visa limits me to only be able to work on-campus). After having several conversations with my advisor, who suggested I speak with the program director about funding sources, I met with the program director and expressed my desire to be a Teaching Assistant (TA) because I did have experience teaching back home and felt I would be able to contribute to the course. I also explained to him that I wasn't allowed to work outside campus due to the visa restrictions. Without a full assistantship, I was concerned that I might not be able to finish the program. However, the program director told me that he was concerned about my accent and my ability to speak English fluently enough to teach. Therefore, he would not give me a Teaching Assistantship. I was really frustrated because another cohort member, who was also a non-native speaker with a strong accent, received a full-assistantship as a TA. Later on, I found out that this TA opportunity went to a native speaking cohort member who already had a full assistantship. I felt I was judged by my language barrier, even though my cohort and clients said they could understand me just fine. I ended up taking more loans than I intended to complete the first year. Eventually my advisor was able to give me a TA opportunity because one of her classes expanded and required a TA. Even though I became a faculty member and have received positive feedback from colleagues and students about my teaching, the conversation I had with the program director has always impacted me, both positively (as a motivation to prove him wrong) and negatively (still think I wasn't good enough).

This is tied to the previous experience that I had with the supervision. When I first started practicum in the summer as a master's student, I was very anxious when I received the feedback from the supervisor that I was "being defensive" about his advice/comment. I met with my advisor, who is also a faculty member in the program. I was almost ashamed to tell her about what happened and that I could not solve the situation on my own since I am an adult. I worried that she would perceive me as incompetent and trouble to the program. But I didn't have any other option but to meet with her as she was my advisor. Therefore, I still met with her and explained to her what happened. She was surprised about the incident and told me that it must have been hard to feel so alone in the situation. I can't recall the details now, but I am pretty sure I started to tear up. She told me that it wasn't my fault that I couldn't keep up with other students and that many international students have struggled with language barriers. We had this long conversation about my ability as a trainee and even the reason I was admitted by the program. This was particularly important for me because I was struggling so much with keeping up in class as well as in practicum. Although I had experiences as a therapist in my home country, doing therapy in English did not come easily. It was frustrating to me because I had ideas to conceptualize my cases but I could not explain it as much as I wanted to others. I could not demonstrate how much I really understood the concepts without thinking about the right vocabulary or the right tense. Having my advisor's feedback allowed me to tell myself that I was admitted by the program because I have potential, not just luck. Her assistance for me to switch groups helped me complete the program on time and continue on to my doctoral degree. I will be forever grateful to have had her as an advisor.

> **Themes**: As an international student, Yang had to navigate the English language as well as American cultural expectations related to participation in graduate education. Her supervisor early on did not grasp the differences between Yang's native culture and American cultural expectations. Other faculty made assumptions about Yang's ability to communicate and relate, based solely on her accent and second language. Like many early career therapists, Yang experienced some self-doubt related to her competency as a therapist, which was compounded by the stereotyping and assumptions of various supervisors and faculty she encountered during graduate school.

Kevin

Kevin is a 35-year-old, naturalized African male, first-generation Ethiopian American, who immigrated from Sudan at six months of age. He studied psychology in undergrad and couples and family therapy in grad school, both at the University of Oregon. He is the first in his family to graduate college. He currently works in an agency, primarily working with children and families of adoption and trauma. Most of his supervisors have been Caucasian, and evenly split between male and female. He currently works with three people of color, and is the only first-generation immigrant in his office.

Keywords: African, Ethiopian, ethnicity/race, first-generation immigrant

My most meaningful experience happened while I was a first-year student, taking the life cycles/stages of life course. I can't recall the exact nature of the assignment, but I know it was related to doing a genogram of our own family. What was particularly challenging about the assignment was reconciling my own relationships with my family. In examining my family dynamics, the weight of the effect of different life events crystallized. I hadn't spent a lot of time trying to understand how I had internalized those events and now I was face to face with them. The support and dialogue the professor allowed for in the course, as well as the nature of how this particular instructor engaged with students, created a safe environment for me to challenge myself to lean into the assignment. The full weight of the assignment didn't really sink in until I approached the instructor to share my appreciation for her approach and how challenging the assignment had been. I began crying, completely unexpectedly. I couldn't even completely give my thanks. The subtle challenge this instructor gave us through our relationship, rather than any overt challenge, had a significant impact on my training. I became more aware of my history, but also came to appreciate the natural healing ability of building relationship as a powerful agent for helping others.

In reflection, I definitely felt more comfortable with the professor because they were a person of color. I think that was definitely influential. Being the only Black male in ALL my classes was isolating at times. That course made me address issues I was having with being SEEN as a Black male, but being raised African, and my parents drawing a distinct difference between the two. The material, projects, and instructor crystallized the struggle I'd had for years with that identity. It gave me a framework to understand the dissonance I'd been feeling and shame associated.

> **Themes**: Kevin's experience as the only Black male in his graduate program, with an intersectional identity inclusive of his African and Ethiopian heritage, as well as his immigrant history, is highlighted in this narrative. Kevin emphasized the importance of critical self-exploration to reconcile the complexities of his lived experiences, ultimately engaging is his own contextual differentiation process. Kevin also had a meaningful experience with a non-judgmental faculty of color who supported him on his journey.

Kimball Hobbs

Kimball is 33 years old and identifies as a cisgender, queer, spiritual, White American female. She is currently able-bodied and connected to middle to upper middle-class contexts. She grew up in both Massachusetts and Florida, attending the University of Florida (public state university) for undergraduate studies, and Seattle University (private Jesuit University) for her master's in MFT. During her years as a trainee and intern, she worked at a community clinic with mostly queer, female-identified clients, as well as couples who identified as both heterosexual and queer. The majority of her supervisors have been White men or women and the majority of her clients have been White women and women of color from lower to middle-class communities.

Keywords: queer, heteronormativity, compartmentalization, dominant discourses

My more challenging experiences have usually been in the classroom. I'm at a Jesuit university so that means my learning environment is shaped by a rather progressive Catholic ethos. As a queer woman, I've been rather surprised by the degree to which I feel acceptance at the school. That being said, I'm ever aware of differing religious perspectives and still feel a need to be careful about how/when/under what circumstances I reveal my sexual orientation. Even in the most progressive spaces, like this one, I always feel a need to be cautious.

In the classroom, as would-be therapists, we learn about relationships, sexuality, systems, and theories. And in my experience, all of these things are looked at through the lens of heteronormativity, with any variation being considered something of an outlier and given a separate chapter. This act of separating, physically placing queer experiences of relationships and sexuality in a separate place in a book, feels like a fairly accurate example of the lived queer experience. To larger society, we exist, but our experiences are so foreign and "odd" that we cannot be placed alongside heterosexuality as a normal experience of sexuality and relationships. I feel like much of my time in the classroom has been about making sure the queer experience is both discussed and normalized.

One of the most meaningful experiences I've had thus far in my training as an MFT was with my current supervisor at my internship site. She, a straight woman, was excited to be working with me, a queer woman, at a clinic that offers counseling to women-identified folks with higher-than-average populations of queer clients. I could understand her excitement because I was able to relate to the clients differently than the straight therapists I was working with. But, because of my life experience that taught me to keep my sexual orientation in the background and not draw too much attention to it, I didn't engage with my own sexual orientation much in our supervision meetings. We would talk about clients and I would talk about transference/counter transference, difficulties, and breakthroughs, but I didn't really discuss how my particular social location impacted my work with clients. Based on my previous encounters with people, I just assumed she didn't want to hear about it.

But one day I was talking about a couple I was seeing—a straight couple—and I mentioned how I was struggling to understand a particular dynamic between the man and woman. I said something like "I feel like I'm missing something, I don't encounter this in my relationship with my wife or any other woman I've dated," and her whole face lit up. She said "finally!" "I've been wanting to hear more about this!" I said, "Really? You've been wanting me to talk about this?" She said "Yes! I want you to be more gay in our supervision meetings. This is who you are and how you'll be relating to your clients." Honestly, I was completely surprised. I'd never heard anyone say "I want you to be more gay." It wasn't until that moment that I'd realized how much of myself I held back from my work, my school—my life. How much I compartmentalize my personal experiences from the outer world and people that I interact with based on the assumption that I won't be accepted or that I'll make other people uncomfortable. It was this amazing realization that I could be my complete self in my work. And it was the first time I'd felt completely seen, understood, and challenged to be more myself by a heterosexual person that wasn't a friend.

Themes: In a heteronormative world, Kimball has learned to compartmentalize her queer identity and leave it in the background as though it is a separate, not "normal" part of her and her relationships. This made her cautious in her training experiences. One heterosexual supervisor encouraged her to bring all of her sociocontextual self into the supervision space and clinical experience. Kimball had the powerful experience of being seen and understood through a supervisory relationship.

Lana Kim

Lana is in her late 30s and identifies as a cisgender, heterosexual, Canadian-born, second-generation woman of Korean descent. She is currently able-bodied. She was born and raised in western Canada to migrant parents from a working class home, and attended the University of British Columbia (public university) for her undergraduate studies and Loma Linda University (private, religiously affiliated, medical and health studies institution) for her master's and PhD in MFT degrees. During her graduate school training, she worked in a variety of settings including an outpatient adolescent unit, community-based integrative health clinic, University-based behavioral health institute, and medical school. She also coordinated state training programs for licensed caregivers and therapists who worked with transitional-aged foster youth. Her supervisors have all been cisgender, heterosexual, White women, but the clientele she has worked with have included people from a wide variety of racial and ethnic identities, sexual identities, gender identities, and socioeconomic backgrounds.

Keywords: Korean Canadian, Asian American, racial identity, decolonization, critical consciousness

What does it take to become a good therapist? Will I be a good therapist? Will clients want to see a therapist like me? When I think back to my earliest years as a trainee, I remember the flood of self-doubt and uncertainty that I felt about whether or not MFT was a viable career path for me. In all honesty, my academic ability and work ethic were not what I questioned. Rather, my anxiety centered around the fear that as an Asian American, my legitimacy as a therapist might be called into question by colleagues, supervisors, and clients alike. I believed that in order to make it, I would have to demonstrate that I could see, think, walk, talk, and do as my supervisors and peers. No one ever said it, but I got the impression that I needed to assimilate as closely as possible to being a White therapist. Based on what I saw represented most in the therapy world, whiteness served as the illusory bar to reach. Over the years, I have often asked myself what this even meant and why I felt such an underlying pressure to prove myself in this way. My initial answer was personal and I assumed that it simply reflected a deficiency on my part—a lack of self-confidence. But, I have since realized that it probably had less to do with my deficiency deficit and more to do with the larger context, and the fact that contextual issues such as color blindness and lack of representation were never acknowledged or discussed during my training.

As a trainee, I was never encouraged or asked to think about my racial identity and how it might intersect with my other identifiers and my developing identity as a family therapist in a field where Asian Americans are highly underrepresented as clinicians, researchers, educators, and as clientele. I had the privilege of learning from a number of brilliant and gifted mentors, and I certainly learned an immense amount of knowledge from them about the practice of family therapy. However, in order to bring my whole self to my practice, I needed opportunities and guidance to: explore what it meant to be a therapist in the context of my racial and bicultural identity; as well as to talk through scenarios I feared I would experience of others perceiving me to have less than full value because of covert biases and prejudices that exist within our society about who is a legitimate therapist. I also needed to see greater difference in the field as a whole. It was through reading literature by authors who wrote from a decolonizing perspective about these deeply personal issues I was wrestling with and connecting with peers and colleagues who also connected to these issues in varying ways that I finally started to see that I had value as a therapist, not in spite of, but because of my social location. Through this, I felt empowered to examine and intentionally construct who I was going to be as a therapist rather than simply aspire to be an honorary White therapist. I believe that we need communities of difference and diverse representation in order to create just training contexts.

> **Themes**: Lana describes how internalizing racism—wondering about her own deficiencies—led to a tumultuous start in the MFT field, filled with much self-doubt and uncertainty. Through engagement with gifted mentors, supportive colleagues, and good decolonizing educational material, she experienced the raising of critical consciousness and empowerment to be a therapist congruent with her social location.

Parvin Saberi-Shakib

Parvin is 27 years old and identifies as a cisgender, heterosexual, U.S.-born, Muslim, second-generation Iranian American female. She is currently able-bodied with a visual disability and connected to middle to upper middle-class contexts. She grew up in both New York City and Los Angeles, attending the University of California, Irvine (public state university) for undergraduate studies, and California State University, Northridge (public state university) for her master's in MFT. During her years as a trainee, she worked at a middle school and high school(s) with students and their families. The majority of her supervisors have been non-White women and the majority of her clients have been Hispanic from lower to working-class communities.

Keywords: Iranian American, Muslim, Islamophobia, otherized, privilege/oppression

As a child of Iranian immigrant parents and a Muslim American that grew up in the shadow of 9/11, I am no stranger to microaggressions; facing discrimination has become a routine part of life. I watched as such Islamophobia became inflamed, normalized, and legitimized during the 2016 US presidential election. I was in my second year of my marriage and family therapy graduate program at the time, and went to school the day after the election feeling distraught and unsafe—both physically as a Muslim that wears the hijab (head covering), and emotionally. I had spent much of the day in a surreal state of mind, oscillating between anger and grief.

I was the only Iranian American Muslim female in my program among predominantly White peers, and never felt more alienated and disconnected from them as I did that day and subsequent weeks. In a private conversation, a classmate told me her good friend had expressed Islamophobic and hateful things, but that she didn't speak up because she didn't want to create conflict and wanted everyone to get along and find common ground. I found myself in the position of comforting and reassuring her despite feeling offended that she didn't use her voice to advocate for someone like me.

My White professor at the time mentioned nothing about the election, did not open any dialogue about the potential discussions we might have with diverse clients affected by the election, or how any individual in the classroom might be affected both personally and professionally. In the following weeks, diversity considerations were ignored completely by my White professors. Finally, a non-White professor checked in with our class about how we were coping with things that were happening in the world. My peers expressed they were tired of people being negative and discussing politics. They murmured in agreement that they found the news too depressing and tried to avoid keeping up with current events as part of their self-care. I felt hurt and disempowered by these words, conscious of the fact that it was such a privilege to choose not to pay attention to the world around you. My peers could simply not relate or understand what a politicized and otherized existence was like on a day to day basis. For me, politics was not just politics, it was deeply personal.

I felt their discussions of self-care lacked acknowledgement of privilege and was afraid of raising my hand to speak up. I was afraid of being judged, and conflicted because I was exhausted from having to be a mouthpiece for an entire minority and heterogeneous group. I felt as if my voice was being silenced. I felt I could not express anger in fear of reinforcing stereotypes about Muslims, afraid of being viewed as too negative. I felt that crucial parts of my identity that were anchored in the development of my identity as a therapist were going unseen and unacknowledged.

Like many other members of minority and othered groups, the results of the 2016 US presidential election left me feeling raw fear, anger, sadness, and disbelief. As an Iranian American Muslim female that lives with a disability, I felt disconnected from my identity as a therapist trainee—how was I supposed to be emotionally present for my clients when I felt emotionally unsafe and unseen as large parts of my identity were walking targets of vindicated hate? This was on my mind as I sat down for my first weekly supervision meeting since election night.

As per usual, my supervisor began our meeting by asking me how I was doing. Although she was Hispanic, I hesitated to be honest because I was fearful of wholly expressing all parts of myself, afraid she would judge my clinical skills and think it was unprofessional to discuss politics. I decided to be candid with her and was met with genuine empathy and understanding. We spent the next hour discussing and processing how we both felt as members of a minority group and clinicians. She listened attentively, normalized and humanized my feelings in context, and clearly acknowledged issues of diversity in that moment.

As a result, I felt inspired to find meaning in my privileged role as a therapist in the following weeks; I formed a support group at the high school where I was completing my traineeship, which predominantly consisted of low-income Hispanic students. My goal was to create a safe space for any student that felt like they needed to process their emotions about any aspect of the political climate that was affecting them. As a young Muslim American growing up in a post 9/11 America, having such a support group would have made all the world's difference to me in feeling accepted and understood. Now, years later, in my professional role as a therapist, I hoped to bridge these parts of myself and make a difference in these students' lives. As I discussed this with my supervisor, she encouraged me, expressed excitement, and supported me completely. I believe that if I didn't have a culturally competent supervisor during this time, it would have left me feeling disempowered and disenchanted.

During the duration of the support group, my clients expressed that they were surprised and relieved that they were not the only ones who were scared or anxious, and afraid of being separated from their undocumented families. They shared similar experiences and expressed they felt inspired, motivated, and empowered because of the group. Facilitating this group was one of the most powerful experiences of my life, and one of the most meaningful and fulfilling experiences I had as a supervisee and trainee. It is an experience I will never forget and one that I could not have had if my supervisor hadn't provided a space that encouraged me to integrate and value all parts of my most authentic self in clinical practice.

> **Themes**: Parvin's experience, post 2016 election, as someone grounded in her Muslim identity, was riddled with uncertainty about relational processes with her faculty and peers in her program and a sense of isolation in her experience of grief and fear. Parvin's critical consciousness about her own experience of disenfranchisement as well as the impact it might be having on those she served in therapy pushed her to find a safe and supportive supervisor with whom to process. Parvin took action, in the midst of her own struggle to advocate and create a socially just space for her clients to share and process.

Peter Mora

Peter is a 27-year-old male, US-born from Mexican descent, and a first-generation college student. Peter was born and raised in Arleta, California and attended San Fernando High School and California State University, Northridge (CSUN). Peter earned a BA in Psychology and an MS in Counseling, with an emphasis in Marriage and Family Therapy. During his years as an MFT trainee and associate, he worked in multiple settings, including court-ordered in-home family treatment for a non-profit, individual therapy in a private practice setting, and group therapy in an intensive outpatient program for high-risk adolescents and young adults. Since becoming a Licensed MFT, Peter is now a Counseling Specialist and adjunct faculty at CSUN, and also has a private practice in Westlake Village, CA. The majority of Peter's supervisors have been White men or women, though his clients/students have ranged from persons of color to White, and lower-middle class families to upper-class families.

Keywords: first-generation student, Mexican American, male, gender, culture

As an intern working in a private setting, a challenge that I encounter in supervision is talking about counter-transference in my individual supervision. I understand processing the material is essential to providing the best possible care for my clients, but I sometimes struggle with knowing whether an issue is counter-transference to be discussed in supervision or an issue I should discuss with my personal therapist. Part of the struggle is that I sometimes believe that I should resolve this issue "like a man," which means one must face the issue straight on instead of going to another person for support. I often feel as if I should already have an answer to my question—sometimes this is in my conscious or subconscious mind.

Although I am fortunate enough to say this challenge rarely comes up, it seems like it's a little different every time I experience it. The last time, I discussed the challenge for me with my supervisor, and as always, he was very encouraging in his thoughts, and even offered to have a full individual supervision session dedicated to the issue in the future. I believe part of this challenge has to do with my perception of being a male supervisee, since in other cases, men are supposed to "deal with it."

Another challenge that I faced as an intern in a group setting is feedback from parents who dismiss the work being done due to being in a non-licensed status. We are fortunate enough to offer family and individual therapy to all our group therapy participants. With such services, comes push back and resistance from parents, and I've often found myself and my colleagues (from parents' point-of-view) as "not knowing what we're doing." This is a very natural part of therapy in any setting, but I struggled with this challenge due to the overwhelming care that my team has for every client.

A challenge that I faced as a student was balancing different responsibilities. As a full-time graduate student, I also held a part-time Student Affairs position on campus, worked as a volunteer In-home Outreach Counselor for a campus community agency, and as an individual therapist at a non-profit counseling center. I was very fortunate to have these positions, but it came with a price of balancing my responsibilities and my personal life (e.g. family, girlfriend, self-care). As a first-generation student, and from a Mexican background which heavily devotes time to family, I struggled with the balancing part. Part of me wanted to spend more time with my family and friends, while another part of me wanted to make sure I reserved enough time to study, do well, and be the first in my family with a college degree. A challenge I encountered was showing parts of my family that they still meant a lot to me while focusing on my studies—all while demonstrating to my schooling colleagues that I was 100% dedicated to the program. I was fortunate to have understanding individuals in both parties; this made it a bit easier, but still difficult nonetheless. Another plus was how my grad school program made sure to mention self-care in—what appeared to be—every single sentence! Making time for myself slowly became a priority on my lists of responsibilities.

As an MFT intern in my clinical setting, I have been blessed with excellent supervision during my time there. A meaningful and fulfilling experience I had as a supervisee included the commitment my supervisor had in one of the toughest cases I have ever been part of. On one specific night, I had a client who appeared to be a danger to himself. Without hesitation, I reached out to my supervisor via text in the middle of my session. The session was taking place in the evening time, well after office hours—yet, my supervisor was quick to respond via phone call, give me directions, and committed to driving over to the agency for an assessment. The reason why this experience was so meaningful to me is because this session came after a demanding week for our agency, yet my supervisor did not hesitate to go the extra mile. This meant a lot to me because it made me feel comfortable in asking for help when I felt it was needed—which is a challenge for me at times. My supervisor's response surprised me not because of his character, but more because of my own personal experience when it comes to asking for help. I have been fortunate enough to have family, friends, and mentors who have been supportive, but for some reason, I still feel like a burden at times. It might be more cultural for me, but it's something I strive to explore in the future. In this case, I came out of my comfort zone, asked for help, and received the best possible response from someone I deeply appreciate and look up to.

Another fulfilling experience I had as a student was finding a chair for my thesis. I felt like I encountered some resistance towards completing a thesis from some of my peers and school faculty—mainly due to its length, need for commitment, and tedious corrections process throughout the experience. As anyone who studies first-generation students can attest, one of the most challenging tasks for a first-gen student to complete is asking for help and not feeling shamed for needing the support. Although no one shamed me, I felt ashamed of asking individuals around me to go an extra mile by chairing a thesis instead of the other options presented to me. I felt like a burden at times, needing somebody to give me "extra" support to complete a personal goal of mine since fifth grade—a sort of selfish endeavor. Much like my experience with my supervisor, sometimes I feel like I should be able to achieve everything I want to achieve on my own. Although I'm not 100% sure why, I do have some thoughts. Growing up, I have already considered myself independent and smart, mostly evidenced by my success in schooling. However, one thing I struggled to be is interdependent, which is a balanced approach between being independent and dependent at the same time—usually the perfect route to take on any task given to you. I struggle with this, partly because of my own expectation of myself (placed on me by no one else but me). It often creates a worry that I may be taking someone else's time, which at my age, can easily be assumed to be more valuable than a beginner in grad school. In spite of these worries, I committed myself to go for the gold while searching for a chair for my thesis. I lobbied prestigious individuals in my MFT program about the possibility of chairing a thesis. It really meant a lot to me when my first choice said yes! The process was easier than I thought due to our commitment, resilience, and dedication. It was such an honor to work with this individual, and it led me to work past my self-perceived limits to complete my graduate thesis.

> **Themes**: Peter's narrative highlights the impact of gendered and cultural expectations related to heteropatriarchy that are situated in both American and Mexican dominant discourses. Specifically, Peter revealed his challenge as a male, to share his personal struggles or to ask for help while in school and during clinical training. Peter's approach increased his own help seeking behaviors which built both his personal confidence as well as clinical confidence. His narrative also underscores the significance of his courage to seek support from trusted supervisors and faculty.

Sam Silverman

Sam is a non-binary Marriage and Family Therapy Associate and an LGBTQ workshop facilitator. They use they/them pronouns. Sam is also White, transgender, able-bodied, queer, and upper middle class. They are currently employed as an associate therapist at an LA-based substance abuse and mental health treatment program for adults. Most of their clients identify as White, cisgender, able-bodied, and LGB. Prior to their current work, they worked in three different locations focusing on substance abuse treatment (two for teens, one for adults), conducted therapy at a junior high school, and conducted individual and family therapy at a training clinic. Sam received their master's in Marriage and Family Therapy from a California State University. For their master's culminating experience, they wrote their final project on trans experiences, providing insight on how to improve the quality of care trans clients receive in therapy. They have given workshops about trans advocacy at Mitchell Family Counseling Clinic, the 2016 EDGY Conference for LGBTQ Youth, The Relational Center, Boeing Aircraft Manufacturing Company, College of the Canyons, Catalyst Con, Sex Positivity Con, and others.

Keywords: gender identity, trans, power/oppression, dismissiveness

My internship is at residential treatment center for teens coping with suicidality and/or drug addiction. When I arrived at the facility I was informed that three of the six current clients identified as trans. During the first group supervision, I introduced myself by "they or them pronouns" and said I was genderqueer. My supervisor said, "we really need you here to help us with this trans stuff." This immediately trivialized my identity and put me in the role of advocate and educator for myself and all trans clients.

During the first staff meeting, the three trans clients' identities became the subject of discussion, in which the validity of each client's identity was questioned. Every therapist in the room consistently misgendered all three trans clients. Multiple therapists and counselors stated that these clients' presentations were "difficult" for them because, for example, the one non-binary client "looked like a girl." Comments like these set the tone for a meeting where cisgender individuals dictated the validity of trans identities.

Workplace interactions became increasingly hostile towards trans individuals. One trans boy was denied access to the boys' bathroom, and body checks (when staff check for sharp objects and drugs on high-risk clients) were performed exclusively by female staff, despite the client's explicit statements that this made him feel uncomfortable and dysphoric. Additionally, weeks were spent discussing what this trans boy should be allowed to wear to go swimming. Because I had been vocal about my own trans identity, multiple staff members asked me what I thought was appropriate swimwear. When I stated that they should "talk to the client directly about his preferences in swimwear," they immediately dismissed this. This signaled to me that trans clients were not granted agency over their own bodies.

I began to engage in explicit discussions with my supervisor about my concerns surrounding these policies. During a meeting, she stated that male staff were concerned about being falsely accused of sexual assault if they were to perform body checks on the trans boy. Another therapist added that she was not sure the client's gender was even real. My supervisor went on to say that the client is manipulative, and therefore his gender identity must be a part of his disorder to get attention. She attempted to explain a clinical basis for this gender invalidation, saying this client sometimes wore short shorts and sometimes showers without resisting and therefore must not really have gender dysphoria. This created a work environment in which the legitimacy of someone else's gender was the subject of debate, which made me feel incredibly unsafe for myself and my clients.

A few days after this meeting where I expressed my concerns, my supervisor met with me to give me a disciplinary notice. It stated that I had behaved "inappropriately" and over-disclosed personal information in the workplace when I politely corrected another staff member on my pronouns. This made it clearer than ever that neither my ethical concerns nor my identity would be treated with respect.

During my second semester as a student and my first semester as a trainee, I took a class called "Diversity in Counseling." This class was taught by a cisgender, heterosexual, White man. Immediately this created a dynamic in which the person in the principal position of power in the classroom to lead discussions about diversity (especially the experiences of marginalized communities in relation to therapy), was also the person with the most privilege in the room. I felt like it was more than likely that I would need to be my own advocate in the classroom.

At this point in my education, I was out about being non-binary, trans, and queer, but was very new to being out about gender and struggling to know how best to advocate for trans-inclusion. During the class, there was a gender section and an LGBT section. In the gender section, the teacher talked about gender as a divide: men vs. women. He also told some sexist jokes that played on gender norms. He made statements implying that all men were male and heterosexual, all women were female and heterosexual, and gender was a binary. The professor went on to speak for and over women in the room. When I spoke to him after class, I told him there were more people than just men and women, and not all men and women adhered to these traditional roles (or slight variations of traditional roles). He expressed no desire to shift his presentation, stating that he was in charge of the class and generalizations are required for teaching this information. When I asked him about the upcoming LGBT section and what would be covered, he stated that a straight cisgender mom would come in to talk about her daughter coming out as a lesbian. When I expressed the desire for myself and other queer individuals in the class to speak about our identities and experiences in therapy, he stated there was no time. When I asked him if the LGBTQ section would discuss trans people at all, he stated that there weren't enough trans people for that to matter and that it wasn't important to cover. I was so upset I could barely speak. I excused myself and left. I had never felt so invalidated. Not only had he stated that my identity was unimportant, he was arguing that it was non-essential for therapists to understand trans clients based on no information on this population whatsoever. I value call-out culture, especially in a therapeutic setting, to counterbalance the unequal differential of power between the therapist and the client or professor and student. Call-out culture means the ability for marginalized folks to bring concerns to people in positions of power or privilege with the hope that people in positions of power or privilege will believe the lived experiences of those marginalized individuals and correct any potentially harmful behaviors without defensiveness or resentments. It is about understanding that those marginalized individuals (in this case trans people) are more familiar with trans experiences and needs than cis people, and that this is okay. It was clear that was not within his comfort zone.

During my second year as a student and my third semester as a trainee, I began working on my final project. At my graduate school, projects are similar to dissertations, except instead of doing research to come to a codified research conclusion, the student conducts an extensive literature review and summarizes research and then uses that research to design some kind of project. In my case, this project took the form of a Trans 101 workshop for therapists. I wanted to pursue this project not only to improve the quality of care trans clients receive, but also to improve the ways that my colleagues and peers scrutinized my own identity as a trans person.

My project advisor, also my supervisor, had discussed the importance of therapeutic work as social justice work. This invoked my curiosity about ways in which activism can be intertwined with therapy in order to advocate for marginalized clients. My advisor helped me mold this idealistic aim of helping trans clients into a realistic and concrete workshop. She also validated how emotionally draining but also meaningful this project was for me because it was so personal. This helped me to push forward. Additionally, gaining concrete statistics, understanding ethical standards, and developing clear syntax to explain the importance of psycho-education for trans clients helped me speak up for myself.

I presented this workshop initially for my colleagues and supervisor at my traineeship. My supervisor gave me the space and time to give that presentation because she understood what that meant to me. Having the opportunity to influence the quality of interactions between myself and my colleagues, as well as the quality of care they provided for trans clients, was incredibly meaningful to me. Through giving a series of workshops and sharing my own identity, I noticed a shift in my colleagues. While they still almost never used my gender pronouns, the way they expressed themselves did change. One colleague's shift was particularly drastic. He went from asking me to tell him about my "crazy wild lesbian sex life" and making jokes about trans women's genitals to correcting a colleague on my pronouns and asking about my unique challenges navigating this program while trans. This was also meaningful in that my supervisor began to acknowledge and correct herself on my pronouns more often than not. This created a more comfortable space for me to talk about and process interactions with my clients, and empowered me to advocate for myself and clients.

> **Themes**: Sam's journey highlights the detrimental impact of a cis centric and binary gender system and the general lack of including trans voices. When oppressive structures operate within the educational and training systems designed to support students, those students with marginalized statuses can choose to be silenced or become burdened to be the advocate for themselves and/or their clients. Sam's own development of critical consciousness related to gender identity and expression empowered them to present their authentic self and to stand up to oppressive supervisors, instructors, and colleagues. Sam's story is one of challenging oppressive dominant discourses regarding gender and highlights the ways in which our work, even as it relates to our own journey, involves advocacy and social justice.

Summary

We appreciate our students' and supervisees' willingness to share their stories. As you have witnessed in this chapter, students with marginalized identities in our field endure and experience the diminishing of their sense of self for many reasons. The MFT training setting offers many intimate spaces—being evaluated in supervision, others observing you conducting therapy, being with clients in their pain. In such spaces, our sociocontextual selves are vulnerable and valuable and we can be given a context in which to flourish or flounder. We hope these stories have given you new ways to reflect on your own experience and courage to persist through your training experience. There is a supervisor, professor, or colleague waiting to see you for your whole self and to encourage you to grow into that fullness.

Questions for Reflection

1. Is there a particular narrative that resonates with you? What do you feel connected with? What are you wondering about?
2. Take time to write your own narrative about a difficult/challenging training experience you have had as a supervisee or student. Share it with someone with whom you can grow together.
3. Take time to write your own narrative about a meaningful/fulfilling training experiences you have had as a supervisee or student. Share it with someone with whom you can grow together.
4. Select a contributor's narrative whose experience and social location are less familiar to you. What do you find yourself wondering about? Reacting to? What would be helpful for you to learn more about and raise your critical consciousness about their particular social location and experience? Are there dominant discourses that you would benefit from deconstructing?

Preparing and Developing the Self-of-the-Trainee

6

This chapter focuses on the importance of developing the self-of-the-trainee as foundational to growth and flourishing as a beginning MFT. It is organized in sections to encourage personal exploration and reflection related to many of the topics introduced in Chapter 1 such as personal social context in connection with larger societal discourses, enhancing critical consciousness, and exploring the impact of power, privilege, and oppression in your life. It is likely that you will engage with these activities with varying levels of interest, stress, reactivity, and concern, all dependent on where you are in your own personal journey of understanding related to your social location and critical consciousness development. We want to normalize the positive aspects of the eye-opening and identity-enhancing activities as well as those that may make you uncomfortable or even uncertain. Whatever your experience, if you participate in these activities with an *open mind*, an *open heart*, and *open hands* you will likely see personal growth and change in your thinking, feelings, and interactions with your *self* and with others over time.

Ethnic minority therapists report that their ethnic identity is an important aspect of their sense of self, influences most every aspect of their experiences, and it is reflected in their overall lifestyle (Wieling & Rastogi, 2003). This indicates that it would be nearly impossible to separate out or close off aspects of your ethnicity when training to become a therapist, and yet, many therapists of color do just that. There is much literature in the field of marriage and family therapy, and mental health fields overall, that emphasizes the importance of personal cultural exploration, but it is not always clear how to do this or why we should do it. So with all the talk in the literature about the cultural self-of-the-therapist, we want to give you an opportunity to examine some of your own layers and how your identity and your experiences intersect with your thoughts, feelings, and actions as a clinician. From this exploration, we hope to embolden you to remain cognizant of those important components of your *self*, and the ways you can, if you are not already, bring those parts into your work as a student, supervisee, and/or therapist.

First, we are going to invite you, the reader, to put your *self* in context. By this we mean to invite you to consider how culture and the many aspects of culture organize your personal, multidimensional identity. As reminder, various aspects of identity are socially constructed, denoting that society has created categories such as race and gender and given them meaning in the context of power, privilege, and oppression (Gergen, 2009). According to McGoldrick, Pearce, and Giordano (2005) culture is one of the most influential determinants of identity. As discussed in Chapter 1, our view of culture is that it is the umbrella that encompasses the intersections of the multiple aspects of our identity: age, ability, ethnicity, gender, indigenous heritage, language, race, religion, sexual orientation, socioeconomic status or social class (and others). Culture invariably shapes the way each of us moves in the world, how we think and feel, and how we respond to and how others respond to us. In Chapter 1 we also mentioned the concept of social location. This chapter will encourage you to consider who you are and how you identify in terms of social location, and the ways in which those parts of your *self* connect to, intersect with, or are influenced by larger societal discourses.

Exploring Our Identity: Who Am I?

The development of *self* is often explained utilizing various frameworks such as Erikson's stages of psychosocial development, Piaget's and Bronfenbrenner's ecological systems theory of human development, and Tajfel's social identity behavioral model (see Bronfenbrenner, 1979; Erikson, 1968; Piaget & Cook, 1952; Tajfel, 1974). The aforementioned developmental models offer explanations for the foundation of various aspects of our *self* identity. Identity development was and continues to be expanded with more models to help us and others to understand more specific and unique aspects of our identity such as: ethnic and racial identity development (for examples see Cross, 1971; Helms, 1995; Phinney, 1989); Biracial and multiracial identity development (see Root, 2003; Wijeyesinghe, 2012); gender identity (see Bem, 1981), and sexual identity (Cass, 1979;

Worthington & Mohr, 2002) to name a few. Models such as the ones listed were created in an effort to help mental health professionals to understand "unique identity development processes as a result of oppression and marginalization" and to encourage us to consider our clients' experiences beyond White or "Eurocentric" frameworks (Shin, 2015, p. 11). We encourage you to explore those models in more depth if you have not; they can expand your ideas and understanding of yourselves (and your colleagues and clients) in context immensely. For the purposes of this book, we will not review those models, but rather refer to aspects of them as we encourage you to consider your own intersectional identity.

Personal Identity Exploration

Numerous scholars in mental health fields emphasize the importance for therapists and therapists in training to have their own awareness of their cultural heritage by engaging in a cultural self-assessment. Hays (2008) created a cultural self-assessment tool to help therapists consider the many aspects of their own converging identity called the ADDRESSING framework: age, developmental disabilities, disabilities acquired, religion and spiritual orientation, ethnic and racial identity, socioeconomic status, sexual orientation, indigenous heritage, national origin, and gender identity (Table 6.1).

One of the activities, suggested by Hays (2008), we like to have our students do is write down this acronym on a piece of paper and put a star next to the letter where one might have a privileged identity. Students often reflect that they are surprised by how many stars they have since many of us, for good reason, tend to have greater consciousness about our oppressed identities. These are some reflections we have heard from students:

- For many students of color who have experienced racial discrimination, it feels incongruent to see themselves with "so many" areas of privilege. They wonder why it's hard to feel as though they have privilege.
- Other students of color also feel empowered in seeing their areas of privilege because they did not have consciousness about oppression of sexual minorities, indigenous peoples, religious minorities, etc. They are grateful for the growing critical consciousness and empathy.
- Students with oppressed identities that are less visible or recognized (such as sexual orientation, disabilities, SES, indigenous heritage, nationality) feel validated and seen as they witness their classmates talk about better understanding their realities.

Table 6.1 ADDRESSING Framework

Age and generational influence	• Chronological age • Life cycle state and developmental tasks • Relevant historical and political influences • Generational cultural norms and values
Developmental disabilities	• Physical, cognitive, mental health conditions • Family rules and expectations about ability • Awareness of and access to resources
Disabilities later acquired	• Physical, cognitive, mental health conditions
Religion and spiritual orientation	• Upbringing and current practices • Fit of orientation with dominant culture • Fit of orientation with family of origin • Risks associated with self-identifying • Benefits of membership
Ethnic and racial identity	• Fluidity vs. static • Personal identity vs. identification by others • Invisible identities; "passing" • Historical perspectives and influences • Impact of immigration, historical trauma
Socioeconomic status (SES)	• Occupation, education, income • Rural, urban, suburban • Family name or status in the community
Sexual orientation/identity	• Fluid vs. static; continuum vs. categories • Interaction with other identity factors • "Outness" and levels of safety
Indigenous heritage	• Context of history, marginalization, power • Self-identity vs. being identified by others • Acculturation; assimilation
National origin	• Immigrants, refugees • Acculturation; assimilation • Language • American assumption
Gender identity	• Roles, expectations, relationship factors • Gender as a continuum rather than binary • Separate from biological sex

Other questions to consider and reflect on, drawn from the University of Michigan (2017) Inclusive Teaching website, to further examine your own ADDRESSING include the following:

1. What part(s) of your identity do you think people first notice about you?
2. What part(s) of your identity are you most comfortable sharing with other people?
3. What part(s) of your identity are you least comfortable sharing with other people?
4. What part(s) of your identity are you most proud of?
5. What part(s) of your identity did you struggle the most with growing up?
6. What part(s) of your identity are the most important to you?
7. What part(s) of your identity are least important to you?
8. What part(s) part of your identity do you feel you face oppression for most often?
9. What part(s) of your identity do you feel you receive privilege for most often?
10. What part(s) of your identity do you think about most as a therapist?
11. Are there part(s) of your identity that you hesitate bringing forward as a therapist with your clients?
    a. As a supervisee with your supervisor(s)?
    b. As a colleague or with your peers?
12. In what ways does your identity have an impact on your interactions with your clients? With your supervisor(s)? With your colleagues or with your peers?
13. For numbers 11 and 12 how does this change when you share important parts of your identity with your client(s)? With your supervisor(s)? With your colleague(s) or peers?

Who Belongs Here: Indigenous and Immigrant Identity

Immigration and status in the United States seem to be hot topics recently, but they have always been part of the backbone of our history. Most of us were taught one perspective of U.S. history—typically a story where the early settlers left persecution in Europe to pursue freedom in a new land. When they arrived on the American continent, they had to go through some wars and fights to figure things out to acquire "free" land, but overall they were courageous pioneers and helpful to the indigenous peoples by bringing their "civilized" ways. What is completely missed and invisible from our education and consciousness is the American history of settler colonialism: "The history of the United States is a history of settler colonialism—the founding of a state based on the ideology of white supremacy, the widespread practice of African slavery, and a policy of genocide and land theft" (Dunbar-Ortiz, 2014, p. 2).

Colonization, the act of carrying out colonialist ideology, begins with a foreign group forcing entry into a geographic territory with the intention to exploit indigenous people's resources. They then establish a society that culturally imposes and disintegrates indigenous culture with the purpose of further dividing the superior colonizer and the inferior colonized. The colonized are depicted as savage and require policing and so a system of domination and oppression is established. The result is a "race-based societal system in which the political, social, and economic institutions in the colony are designed to benefit the colonizer and continually subjugate the colonized" (David & Okazaki, 2006, p. 3).

In U.S. history, this began with the taking of land and destroying of cultures of indigenous peoples. The mentality that colonizers rightfully own the land, are superior to, and need to protect what they have conquered is what undergirds the country's relationship with immigrants and "outsiders." Time and again, laws and acts were put into place to exclude, subjugate, imprison, put into camps, and kill/lynch those who were perceived as not belonging.

The resulting colonial mentality impacts every one of us, whether or not we identify as indigenous, immigrant, citizen, or undocumented. This shared consciousness (or unconsciousness rather) finds its way into how we think, breathe, and live. This mentality is a pervasive internalized oppression that leads colonized people to believe we are inferior to the colonizers, who represent whiteness and Western culture. We strive to be "like them" (have lighter skin, bigger eyes, English fluency/no accent) and to belong, so there are parts of who we are that we learn to detest.

David and Okazaki (2006) constructed a Colonial Mentality Scale (CMS) for Filipino Americans and the statements are helpful for considering our own colonial mentality. In place of "Filipino," you can think of your own cultural/ethnic background.

- There are situations where I feel inferior because of my ethnic/cultural background.

- In general, I feel that being a person of my ethnic/cultural background is not as good as being White/European American.
- I feel that there are very few things about the Filipino culture that I can be proud of.
- In general, Filipino Americans should be thankful and feel fortunate for being in the United States.
- I find persons who have bridged noses (like Whites) as more attractive than persons with Filipino (flat) noses.
- I would like to have skin-tone that is lighter than the skin-tone I have.
- I do not want my children to be dark-skinned.
- I think newly-arrived immigrant Filipinos are backwards, have accents, and act weird.
- I think newly arrived immigrants should become Americanized as quickly as possible (David & Okazaki, 2006, p. 245).

Having a colonized mentality translates into self-perceptions and self-doubt for beginning MFTs. We are typically being assessed by or measuring ourselves against a White Western heteronormative way of "doing therapy." It is important to embark on the continual journey of decolonizing our minds so that we can do this with our clients.

Exploring Race and Racial Identity

In their work emphasizing the importance of MFTs taking steps toward greater racial awareness, Hardy and Laszloffy (2008) encourage therapists to explore their own racial identity. The examination of one's own racial identity starts with the first step of acknowledging that race matters and is a major structure of American society. Another step is to recognize that because race does matter, we must acknowledge structural inequalities in society that are grounded in the construction of race which result in privilege and oppression. Another step in the process of developing more racial awareness involves taking proactive steps to engage with racially diverse people. Then, the authors suggest individuals answer the following questions: What does it mean to identify with my racial identity? What implications does my racial identity have for my relationships with others who are racially similar or different? Finally, similarly to many of the discussions that will follow, individuals must inventory the ways in which they are oppressed by and benefit from as well as perpetuate, often unconsciously, oppressive forces operating in our society. This activity could be utilized in the examination of other socially constructed aspects of your identity as well.

Another exercise suggested by Tatum (1997) is to consider your first race-related memory. Take some time to think about and maybe even write about the following questions. How old were you? What do you remember? Was it related to something someone said or did? Were you the observer or the observed? What feelings do you recall? Did you talk to anyone about what happened? If yes, who and why? If not, why not? Take time to reflect on how your earliest race-related experience may have been different if you identified or looked different than you do. Also consider the historical context of your memory: What was happening in the space where you were living? What was happening socially and politically? What is the same or different now?

Gender, Patriarchy, and Sexism

In this section we mean to focus on gender in terms of identity, power, and privilege, with a brief exploration of feminism. We are going to utilize social justice advocate, Sam Killermann's widely accessible information from itspronouncedmeterosexual.com, to briefly review definitions for the concepts of sex, gender identity, and gender expression. Sex is typically assigned male, female, or intersex at birth and is determined based on sexual organs, hormones, and chromosomes. The sex assigned at birth can significantly contribute to gender identity formation, at least early in development. Gender identity is a social construction, not based in biology but often influenced by it, regarding the state of who a person thinks they are: as male, female, or somewhere on a continuum that includes gender nonconforming, genderqueer, agender, or bigender, etc. Our gender identity is informed by biology (hormones) as well as social, cultural, and familial environment. Gender expression is the way in which we enact or represent our gender identity such as dress, hairstyle, and behavior. Gender expression can also be explained on a continuum from masculine to feminine with androgynous in the middle.

A person who is born with male reproductive organs at birth, who identifies as male, and expresses himself in a masculine way would likely be considered cisgender. Cisgender individuals benefit from power and privilege that comes with "normalized" meanings that construct gender (Sorrells, 2016). Inherent in discussions of gender identity and expression are the concepts of power, privilege, and oppression. In most societies around the world, "women and their social, economic, and political roles are inevitably devalued" (p. 57) and transgender or third gender people are pathologized or erased. Linked to the discussion of gender are patriarchy, sexism, feminism, and gender equity.

Patriarchy is a form of social organization based on the presumption and centering of cisgender males "as strong, capable, wise, and composed" while "the female gender is perceived as weak, incompetent, naive, and confused" (Arvin, Tuck, & Morrill, 2013, p. 13; Sorrells, 2016). Heteropatriarchy is a concept rooted in the male/female binary, that privileges cisgender males/masculinity and heterosexual domestic arrangements. Feminism, then, began as a response to challenge the marginalization and oppression of women (when gender was still considered binary) or gender equality (Robinson-Wood, 2017). Feminism is complex and has a second, third, and fourth wave as well as many critiques by native women and women of color, which is well beyond the scope of this book. So, when we refer to feminism, we acknowledge the complexity of what it means to suggest its singular focus on gender issues and sexism. Feminism as we are thinking about it is centered in women's issues or sexism, but does not exclude how women's issues intersect with and are affected and complicated by race, class, religion, sexual orientation, and trans rights.

For reflection in this section, spend time thinking about the gender messaging you have received. What were you taught about what it means to be male or female? Who taught you these ideas? Family? Friends? Religion? How do you believe the messages you have received about gender and gender expression have been influenced by sexism? Patriarchy? How do you understand your own gender identity? In what ways do you express masculine and feminine traits? How has your understanding and expression of your gender identity been supported by those close to you? Society? In what ways does/will your gender identity and expression interact with your role as a therapist? What concerns you?

For those of you who may want to explore these concepts or ideas beyond the explanations and suggestions above, the following are some recommendations.

Explore Gender Socialization with the following documentaries and book:	• *The Mask You Live In* written, directed, and produced by Jennifer Siebel Newsom • *Miss Representation* written, directed, and produced by Jennifer Siebel Newsom • *A Guide to Gender: The Social Justice Advocate's Handbook* by Sam Killermann
Explore Sexism and Male Privilege with the following TED Talks and at www.wearemanenough.com:	• *A Call to Men* • *Why Gender Equality is Good for Everyone—Men Included* • *Man Enough*
Explore Feminism with the following books:	• *We Should All Be Feminists* by Chimamanda Ngozi Adichie • *Feminism is for Everybody: Passionate Politics* by bell hooks

Genograms

Genograms are a visual representation, typically utilized by therapists with clients, to track family patterns, history, and relationships originally created by early family therapy pioneer Murray Bowen (McGoldrick, Gerson, & Petry, 2008). They are commonly used during the assessment phase of therapy to gather family information in one place. Genograms can be updated with more details as the therapist learns more about various family members, relationships, and other factors. Genograms traditionally include the immediate and extended family (typically three generations) with names, ages, gender, relationship status, relational patterns (e.g. close, overly close, conflictual, etc.), medical and mental health status, and important dates such as marriage, divorce, and death. Over time, the use of genograms continuously evolves and more information can be included such as education, work and career, more detailed medical history, sexual history and sexuality, spirituality and religion, and culture and cultural stories. Genograms can also be especially useful for student therapists for their own personal growth, development, and understanding. For the purpose of this book, we are going to examine two subgenres of the genogram: the cultural genogram and the critical genogram.

Cultural Genograms

Hardy and Laszloffy (1995) introduced cultural genograms to help developing therapists examine and come to a deeper understanding of their own cultural identity and to increase multicultural awareness. In their work, Hardy and Laszloffy (1995) distinguish between cultural awareness and cultural sensitivity. Awareness involves our exposure to content about various aspects of *other* cultural groups while sensitivity is focused on our personal connection to *our own* cultural groups and background. The added layer of sensitivity pushes us to consider how our own culture and identities intersect with our understanding of other cultures and identities. Hardy and Laszloffy specifically state,

> Awareness is primarily a cognitive function; an individual becomes conscious of a thoughts or action and processes it intellectually. Sensitivity, on the other hand, is primarily an affective function; an individual responds emotionally to stimuli with delicacy and respectfully... Essentially awareness involves a conscious sensitivity, and sensitivity involves a delicate awareness.
>
> (pp. 227–228)

Cultural genograms can be a tool used to incite cultural awareness and sensitivity for early career therapists by encouraging closer examination of their own cultural identities. Cultural genograms encourage students to look at the intersections of family-of-origin issues and how they intersect with culture: race, class, gender, ethnicity, sexual orientation, religion, etc. Cultural genograms can serve as an eye-opening experience for all therapists, especially since there is no avoiding culture, as some White individuals will say: *I don't have a culture* when in fact everyone is located somewhere on the dimensions of race, class, gender, religion, and sexual orientation (Hardy & Laszloffy, 2008). Cultural genograms (see example in Figure 6.1) push therapists to understand themselves individually as persons with culture and they help therapists to understand how their own cultural and family patterns are tied together. When therapists connect more deeply and authentically with their cultural selves, they feel encouraged to engage more openly with their clients around their clients' cultural identities (Hardy & Laszloffy, 2008; Keiley et al., 2002).

Developing the Self-of-the-Trainee   117

Steps for completing a cultural genogram include:

1. Defining one's culture of origin, meaning the major racial or ethnic groups from which one has descended.

    a. You can expand culture to religious group, if that is a major component of your identity.

2. Identifying organizing principles for each group, which shape the perceptions, beliefs, and behaviors of the group.
3. Identifying pride and shame issues for each group, which punctuate behaviors as negative and positive.
4. Creating symbols for pride and shame issues.
5. Selecting colors to represent each group comprising the individual's culture of origin.
6. Putting together with a key or cultural framework chart.

Upon completion of the cultural genogram, it would be beneficial to share the genogram in a safe space, such as a class, practicum, or even

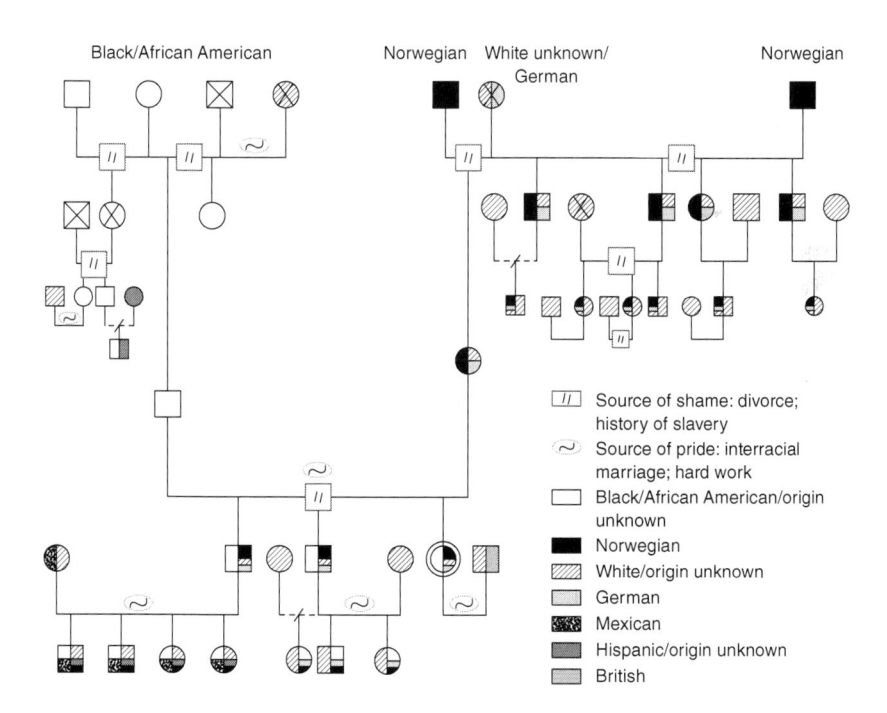

Figure 6.1 Genogram 1

supervision. In the event sharing is not possible, the following are questions from Keiley and colleagues (Keiley et al., 2002, p. 169; 176) and Hardy and Lasloffy (1995), for your personal reflection. In terms of gender: What role does gender play in terms of "keepers" of your culture(s)? Are there gender differences related to cultural expectations or pride and shame issues? What are your experiences of being an oppressor and/or the oppressed in your culture and how has your gender influenced these experiences? At the completion: What aspects of the cultural genogram were most valuable to you? Why were they valuable? What was your experience constructing the genogram? How do you think your experience constructing and examining your cultural genogram will impact your work with clients? (See Table 6.2 and Table 6.3.)

Table 6.2 Questions to Consider While Preparing for the Cultural Genogram Presentation

Please consider these questions for *each* group constituting your culture of origin, as well as considering the implications of the answers in relation to your overall cultural identity.

1. What were the migration patterns of the group?
2. If other than Native American, under what conditions did your family (or their descendants) enter the United States (immigrant, political refugee, slave, etc.)?
3. What were/are the group's experiences with oppression? What were/are the markers of oppression?
4. What issues divide members within the same group? What are the sources of intra- group conflict?
5. Describe the relationship between the group's identity and your national ancestry (if the group is defined in terms of nationality, please skip this question).
6. What significance does race, skin color, and hair play within the group?
7. What is/are the dominant religion(s) of the group? What role does religion and spirituality play in the everyday lives of members of the group?
8. What role does regionality and geography play in the group?
9. How are gender roles defined within the group? How is sexual orientation regarded?

(Continued)

Table 6.2 (Cont.)

10. a) What prejudices or stereotypes does this group have about itself? b) What prejudices and stereotypes do other groups have about this group? c) What prejudices or stereotypes does this group have about other groups?
11. What role (if any) do names play in the group? *Are* there rules, mores, or rituals governing the assignment of names?
12. How is social class defined in the group?
13. What occupational roles are valued and devalued by the group?
14. What is the relationship between age and the values of the group?
15. How is family defined in the group?
16. How does this group view outsiders in general and mental health professionals specifically?
17. How have the organizing principles of this group shaped your family and its members? What effect have they had on you?
18. What are the ways in which pride/shame issues of each group are manifested in your family system?
19. What impact will these pride/shame issues have on your work with clients from both similar and dissimilar cultural backgrounds?
20. If more than one group comprises your culture of origin, how were the differences negotiated in your family? What were the intergenerational consequences? How has this impacted you personally and as a therapist?

Table 6.3 Questions to Answer in Synthesis Paper

1. What are your family's beliefs and feelings about the group(s) that comprise your culture of origin? What parts of the group(s) do they embrace or reject? How has this influenced your feelings about your cultural identity?
2. What aspects of your culture of origin do you have the most comfort "owning," the most difficulty "owning"?
3. What groups will you have the easiest time working with, the most difficult?
4. What did you learn about yourself and your cultural identity? How might this influence your tendencies as a therapist?
5. Was the exercise valuable, worthwhile? Why or why not?

Critical Genograms

Critical genograms were conceptualized as tools to aid MFTs in their journey to becoming critically conscious (see example in Figure 6.2). The critical genogram or CritG, as utilized by the authors Kosutic and colleagues (2009), pushes therapists to map the influence of racism, sexism, and classism on their individual and family identities. When MFTs consider the individual and familial impact of these larger sociopolitical systems and historical contexts, they may develop sensitivity and take action to effect change related to the politics of social location. Drawing on the discussion of critical consciousness from previous chapters, when you are actively developing critical consciousness you are reflecting on how power, privilege, and oppression intersect with your own lives and larger social systems and you are taking action to resist those dominant social and political structures (Kosutic et al., 2009).

A CritG is constructed in three parts: developing a basic genogram, drawing systems of oppression, and using reflective questions to facilitate discussion and exploration of the genogram (Kosutic et al., 2009). Sociopolitical contexts, such as age, gender, sexuality, class, race, ability, religion, etc., should be considered to help you identify systems of oppression that are most salient in your life. A CritG can be constructed using paper or a computer along with various shapes and colors to represent various contexts and social forces that may be operating in your family of origin. Geometric shapes such as rectangles or triangles may be used to represent social structures that impact or have a significant role in the family. You can then add in symbols, similar to a regular genogram, that denote closeness and conflict between individuals and communities, social groups, or nations, for example. Then arrows and boxes may be used to indicate resources and power while pie charts can be used to represent power relations, privilege, and exploitation.

> **Ideas for Diagramming Systems of Oppression**
>
> *Geometric shapes.* Geometric shapes may serve to denote each of the larger social structures that play a role in a particular family.
> *Symbols for closeness and conflict.* Symbols for closeness and conflict (McGoldrick, Gerson, & Petry, 2008) may be used to depict relational dynamics among larger social structures. That is, although they are traditionally used to represent relationships among individual

human beings, symbols for closeness and conflict may also be used to depict relationships among communities, social groups, or nations, or relationships between individuals and larger social entities.

Arrows and boxes. Arrows and boxes may be used to represent differential access to resources and power among larger social entities and among individuals. Thicker arrows may be used to indicate more power and/or greater access to resources, whereas thinner arrows may be used to indicate less power. Boxes may be used to indicate the mechanism of domination that operates in a particular situation. Even in families where all members belong to the same category of difference (e.g., the same ethnicity, the same religion, or the same nation of origin), arrows and boxes could be used to show privilege and subjugation.

Pie charts. Like arrows and boxes, pie charts could be used to depict power relations, privilege, and exploitation. Pie charts may also be used to highlight change or instability. For instance, a series of pie charts along a vertical timeline may be used to indicate the changing nature of race relations within a given social context.

Kosutic et al. 2009, pp. 175-176

When the CritG is used within MFT training programs, the authors recommend that each person first reflect on their own CritG and then present the CritG to a safe group of peers. The purpose of sharing the CritG is to experience "support, acceptance, and validation" balanced with a challenge to our own world views and experiences of power and privilege (p. 161). Since the creation of your own CritG may be something you do on your own, and not within the space of a supportive group, we recommend you spend time in self-reflection and journaling to deepen your understanding and critical consciousness.

Reflective Questions for Constructing the CritG[1]

As you are constructing the critical genogram, think about the following questions for each aspect of your social identity and axis of your social location (e.g., race, gender, ability, sexual orientation, class, ethnicity, religion, etc.).

Not all the questions may apply to you. Please record (and answer) the questions that you feel are particularly relevant to the exploration of your own critical genogram. If any of the questions below trigger you in some way, take notice of this reaction and of the question that triggered it.

1. What *markers of oppression/privilege* are associated with this axis of your social location? For example, in relation to race, what is the significance of skin color and hair in the United States? How about in other countries where you may have lived? In relation to gender, how has gender been "done" across generations and contexts, and how have gender roles been defined in your social context? In relation to sexuality, how has it been constructed in your family (and in your country) and how does that relate to gender expectations?
2. In what ways have you *benefited from or experienced marginalization* based on this aspect of your social location? For example, how does the heterosexual norm affect your life and work?
3. What is your experience of *being the oppressor or the oppressed* in a particular context in relation to a given aspect of your social location?
4. How did your *family, community, and the media define this aspect of your social location* at various points in your life (e.g., childhood, adolescence, adulthood)? What positive or negative messages did you receive? What are your earliest images of this aspect of your social location? For instance, what are your earliest images of race? How did your family respond to racism/sexism/discrimination? How did you make meaning of it as part of your social location?
5. What are your *feelings during interactions* with those who share this aspect of social identity? Alternatively, what are your feelings about the absence of interacting with those who share a social identity? What are your feelings during interactions with those who do not share this aspect of social identity? What, if anything, do these interactions affect the way you feel about yourself?
6. What specific *pride or shame issues* are associated with this aspect of your social identity? That is, what aspects of your social identity do you have the most comfort "owning," or the most difficulty "owning"? In what ways did your family, community, and society influence your pride or shame?

7. What role does *migration* play in the (re)construction of this aspect of your social identity? For example, how does your racial identity vary across national contexts? Another example would be the role of changing demographics within your community (due to global or regional migration) on the reconstruction of your social identity.
8. How have *differences* based on various aspects of social location been negotiated within your family, community, or nation? For example, are there people of different ethnicities in your family and, if so, how are these differences negotiated? How has that influenced you?
9. What role does *colonization* play in shaping your social location?

Questions for Guiding Follow-Up Reflection

Having constructed a critical genogram, think about the following questions. Not all questions may be relevant to you.

1. In what ways have your ancestors used race, economics, gender, and politics to foster (i.e., justify, support, maintain) both past and present-day disparities? In what ways have you used race, economics, gender, and politics to foster both past and present-day disparities within a particular social context?
2. In what ways have your accomplishments and your ancestors' accomplishments benefited others or been at others' expense?
3. In what ways do you fulfill your moral obligation to correct current social inequities? Are these ways meaningful to those who have been wronged or just meaningful to you?
4. How do you demonstrate callousness either overtly (e.g., demanding that those without boots or straps pull themselves up by their bootstraps) or covertly (e.g., championing more materials for "gifted" students while ignoring the needs of students who lag behind)?
5. What groups do you have the easiest time working with? The most difficult? What makes the group(s) easy or difficult to work with?
6. In what ways do your reactions of fear, avoidance, and devaluation of this process derail your progress toward socializing your critical consciousness?

Kosutic et al. 2009, pp. 174-175

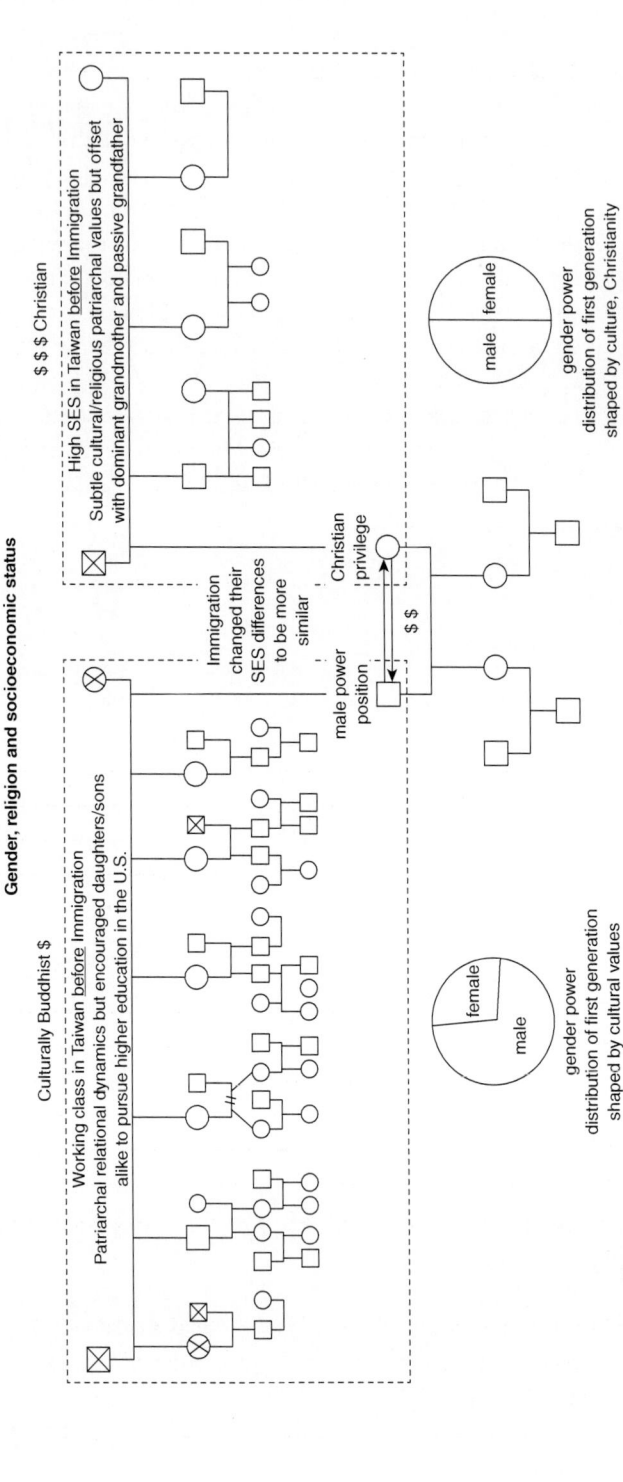

Figure 6.2 Genogram 2

Considering Diversity in Our Lives

One aspect of diversity that we do not always consider is that of our surroundings. With whom we choose to spend time or who is in the spaces we frequent can tell us something about our preferences and possibly what or who helps us to feel comfortable. Sometimes taking note of different aspects of our surroundings can tell us something about our intercultural or multicultural experiences as well as our tendency toward homogeneous environments. As noted above, Hardy and Laszloffy (2008) as well as many other scholars emphasize the importance of exposing ourselves to diverse people and immersing ourselves into diverse experiences. But sometimes, unless we take time to notice the environments in which we live, work, and play, we may not recognize or realize the extent of homogeneity in which we are immersed. The following is a checklist for you to consider. For the following prompts, think about ability, age, gender, language, race/ethnicity, religion, sexual orientation, SES, and veteran status.

In my environment:

I am _____.
My family members are mostly_____.
Other people who live in my home are mostly _____.
My close friends are mostly _____.
People who regularly visit my home are mostly _____.
My neighbors are mostly _____.
My colleagues are mostly _____.
My supervisor is _____.
My graduate institution is mostly _____.
My professors are mostly _____.
My cohort is mostly _____.
My dentist is _____.
My doctor is _____.

After completing the sentence prompts, use these questions for consideration and reflection.

1. Am I someone who actively seeks intercultural experiences?
2. Am I someone who regularly engages in intercultural exchanges with others?

---

3. What is something about my surroundings that I had not noticed before?
4. What is one way I would like to enrich my cultural environment and/or exchanges?
5. How might my answers to each of the preceding questions impact my work with peers in my MFT program? My supervisors? The clients I am or will be working with?

Where are You on a Continuum of Racism and What You are doing about It?

When considering the -isms- racism, sexism, classism, ableism, heterosexism, etc. we often think of ourselves as we are (insert racist, sexist, etc.) or we are not. In other words, the -isms are oftentimes thought of in terms of an either–or dichotomy (Heinze, 2008). As noted by Heinze, it would be more common for people, White people in particular, to not think of themselves as racist or having racist thoughts. In fact, it would be quite courageous for a White person to admit that they might hold racist thoughts at all. Heinze centers his conception of a continuum of racism within the context of White racial awareness. If White folks do not have a sense of themselves as "white" or as belonging to a cultural group, it would be more difficult to acknowledge that White folks do in fact have White privilege and do in fact hold racist thoughts, even if they are unconscious. The purpose of examining our own White privilege and racism is about "learning not knowing." This means that White people are born benefiting from racism but are typically not conscious of the benefit (Helms, 1995). So when White people become conscious, they do not necessarily know or understand all the ways they may benefit from or even perpetuate racism, but rather begin a lifelong journey of learning how they benefit from and perpetuate racism. During the journey, it is also important for White people to confront their feelings of guilt as well as feelings of entitlement and superiority, within safe spaces, for a deeper impact on their development (Wilkins et al., 2013). This journey, for those who become critically conscious, will also likely involve your consideration of what role you want to take in dismantling structural inequality and the perpetuation of racism. At the start of this paragraph we mentioned other -isms that are important to examine as well. We hope you will also take time to think about where you are on a continuum of ableism, ageism, anti-Semitism, audism, classism, colonialism, colorism, ethnocentrism, heterosexism, racism, sexism, sizeism, and xenophobia, etc. and to consider your own privilege in terms of each; the ways in which you might perpetuate heterosexist or ableist, etc. thoughts, attitudes, or behaviors; and what you are doing to dismantle or to disrupt the perpetuation of each.

Implicit Bias

The Implicit Association Test (IAT) measures attitudes and beliefs that may be unconscious or that people may not want to share with others. This project started among a group of scientists who were interested in understanding implicit social cognition. At a very basic level, "the IAT measures the strength of associations between concepts and evaluations or stereotypes" (Project Implicit, 2011). Stereotypes, which are overgeneralized beliefs about people or things, are unconscious or automatic thoughts and are the "implicit" in IAT. Social or implicit cognition is the idea that people's behaviors are influenced by some past experience; but typically that experience is not remembered explicitly or consciously (Greenwald & Banaji, 1995). The purpose of Project Implicit is to educate the public about hidden biases. Important to note is that awareness of biases does not necessarily mean that an individual is prejudiced. Oftentimes, our preferences for one group over another is contrary to what we consciously think and believe. When our biases are revealed after taking one of the tests, it is an opportunity to examine where those implicit attitudes may have come from and what you can do to change implicit biases you do not want operating in your mind. The tests cover a range of topics including skin-tone, sexuality, race, weight, and Arab-Muslim to name a few. We encourage all of our readers to visit the website for Project Implicit (https://implicit.harvard.edu) and to take one or more of the tests available to increase your own awareness and understanding of your implicit biases. In particular we want to encourage you to engage with those surveys that you may be most challenged by or for which you may have known or assumed bias.

International Student Experiences

The research on the experiences of international students in the field of marriage and family therapy is limited. However, the experiences of the international student in MFT graduate programs and in their clinical training in the field is certainly unique. International trainees have many aspects of their own identity and journey to explore that are often overlooked, or at least not a central focus when it comes to education and training. Here we want to create a space for the international student to explore aspects of their own development as a therapist, while traversing cultures, while at the same time we would like to encourage readers who do not identify as international to reflect on the ways in which your graduate program or training has integrated (or not) the experiences of international students. In their qualitative research study on the training experiences of international doctoral students in marriage and family therapy programs, Mittal and Wieling (2006) made several recommendations for MFT training programs to consider. We have reviewed their research study and adapted their findings into a series of reflection questions.

1. In what ways do you experience your graduate program as an "outsider"?
2. What adjustments have you had to make, to adapt to the cultural context of graduate school in the United States? Are there shifts or adjustments that are still a struggle for you?
3. How does your proficiency in English affect your sense of confidence in the classroom and with school work? In supervision or with clients?
4. How does the location of your graduate program (e.g. urban/rural, private/public) promote or hinder your experiences as an international student and as a trainee?
5. In what ways does your graduate program include and exclude other cultural and international perspectives in their education and training?
6. In what ways have you been able to bring your unique perspective and experiences from your country of origin into the classroom? Supervision? Your work with clients?
7. In what ways have you felt limited or discouraged from bringing in the unique aspects of your culture or country of origin into your education and training?
8. In what ways have the program faculty and students supported you? Are there things they could do better?
9. What are things you would like to share with your faculty and cohort, to help them understand how you will use/adjust/adapt your education in MFT when you return to your country of origin?

Heteronormativity, Heterosexism, Homophobia, and Sexual Orientation

Just as we must examine our racial selves and our gendered selves, we must also consider ourselves in terms of our own sexual orientation and our comfort level, biases, values, and prejudices regarding the sexual orientation of ourselves and others (Rock, Carlson, & McGeorge, 2010). Sexual orientation refers to romantic, sexual, or emotional attraction to another person (Thomas & Schwarzbaum, 2017). Sexual identity refers the way(s) in which people choose to identify as it relates to their sexual orientation. As with other identity statuses, an individual may have same-sex romantic and sexual attraction and relationships but may not select a lesbian, gay, bisexual, or queer (LGBQ) identity as a primary identifier. For the purposes of our book, we want to encourage you to consider your own development and understanding of your sexual orientation and identity and then also to consider the ways in which our heteronormative, and oftentimes heterosexist culture, have supported or deterred your own development and personal views. For brief review: heteronormativity is the assumption of heterosexuality or opposite sex sexual attraction and relationships as universal or the norm (Sorrells, 2016). Heteronormative assumptions contribute to the invisibility of LGBQ individuals (McGeorge & Carlson, 2011). Heterosexism is institutional and systemic oppression "that denies and denigrates nonheterosexual behavior, identity, or community" (p. 105). Homophobia is the enactment and perpetuation of irrational dread or fear of homosexuality (Thomas & Schwarzbaum, 2017).

The following questions are adapted from Thomas and Schwarzbaum's (2017) clinical applications for working with individuals regarding their sexual orientation (p. 351) as well as McGeorge and Carlson's sample questions for exploring heteronormative assumptions (p. 17). We encourage you to take some time to reflect on the following questions for yourself.

1. What did your family of origin teach you about sexual orientation, identity, and attraction?
2. What did or does your religious or spiritual community teach you about sexual orientation and sexual identity?
3. Which sex or sexes are you attracted to, do you fantasize about, engage in sexual relations with?

> 4. Can you recall when and/or how you came to understand your sexual orientation?
> 5. How do you label or identify yourself in terms of your sexual identity/orientation?
> 6. With whom do you feel comfortable talking about, sharing with, or relating to regarding your sexual identity/orientation?
> 7. What fears or shame do you experience related to your sexual identity/orientation?
> 8. What messages have you received from your family and society about *your* sexual orientation/identity? What about sexual orientation or identity that differ from yours?
> 9. What messages have you received from your family and society about sexual orientation and identity that does not fall within a heteronormative framework?
> 10. In what ways do you perpetuate heterosexist biases and heterosexual privilege?
> 11. To what extent do you support or advocate for LGBQ rights?

Communication Styles

Something we have witnessed and also experienced is how varying communication styles (often related to our social location) impact connection to one another. There are many communication styles and scales that we would encourage you to explore, but we wanted to focus on the High- and Low-Context Communication continuum. This way of conceptualizing human communication assumes that it is dependent on contextual variables such as culture (individualism/collectivism, race, language, etc.), the physical environment (actual location of the interaction), socio-relational variables (boss/employee, spouse/partner, professor/student), and perceptual variables (attitudes, emotions) (Neuliep, 2012). How each of us focuses on these contexts during communication can vary widely.

High-context cultures emphasize the contextual variables of communication.

> The rules for communication are implicit, and communicators are expected to know and understand unspoken communication. High-context communication involves using and interpreting messages

that are not explicit, minimizing the content of verbal messages, and being sensitive to the social roles of others.

(Neuliep, 2012, p. 63)

High-context cultures tend to have collectivistic values. Low-context cultures focus more on what is verbalized as the primary way that information is imparted and tend to have individualistic values.

Moreover, the rules and expectations are explicitly outlined. [Communicators] are dependent on words to convey meaning and may become uncomfortable with silence. In low-context transactions, the communicants feel a need to speak. People using low-context communication are expected to communicate in ways that are consistent with their feelings.

(Neuliep, 2012, p. 63)

This is a very general introduction to High- and Low-Context Communication styles. On the survey below, you can get a sense of where you might fall on the High to Low-Context Communication scale. Whether in the classroom, between therapist and client, supervisor and supervisee, we believe understanding ourselves and others' communication styles can help us to be more empathic instead of judgmental. A low-context communicator might assume that a high-context communicator is less intelligent or not competent when the high-context communicator is trying to be respectful to their superior. Conversely, a high-context communicator might perceive a low-context communicator to be abrasive or intrusive by their direct way of speaking.

Low- and High-Context Communication Scale

Directions: Below are 32 statements regarding how you feel about communicating in different ways. In the blank to the left of each item, indicate the degree to which you agree or disagree with each statement. If you are unsure or think that an item does not apply to you, enter a 5 in the blank.
Strongly Disagree 1 2 3 4 5 6 7 8 9 Strongly Agree

_____ 1. I catch on to what others mean, even when they do not say it directly.
_____ 2. I show respect to superiors, even if I dislike them.
_____ 3. I use my feelings to determine whether to trust another person.
_____ 4. I find silence awkward in conversation.
_____ 5. I communicate in an indirect fashion.
_____ 6. I use many colorful words when I talk.
_____ 7. In argument, I insist on very precise definitions.
_____ 8. I avoid clear-cut expressions of feelings when I communicate with others.
_____ 9. I am good at figuring out what others think of me.
_____ 10. My verbal and nonverbal speech tends to be very dramatic.
_____ 11. I listen attentively, even when others are talking in an uninteresting manner.
_____ 12. I maintain harmony in my communication with others.
_____ 13. Feelings are a valuable source of information.
_____ 14. When pressed for an opinion, I respond with an ambiguous statement/position.
_____ 15. I try to adjust myself to the feelings of the person with whom I am communicating.
_____ 16. I actively use a lot of facial expressions when I talk.
_____ 17. My feelings tell me how to act in a given situation.
_____ 18. I am able to distinguish between a sincere invitation and one intended as a gesture of politeness.
_____ 19. I believe that exaggerating stories makes conversation fun.
_____ 20. I orient people through my emotions.
_____ 21. I find myself initiating conversations with strangers while waiting in line.
_____ 22. As a rule, I openly express my feelings and emotions.
_____ 23. I feel uncomfortable and awkward in social situations where everybody else is talking except me.
_____ 24. I readily reveal personal things about myself.
_____ 25. I like to be accurate when I communicate.
_____ 26. I can read another person "like a book."
_____ 27. I use silence to avoid upsetting others when I communicate.
_____ 28. I openly show my disagreement with others.
_____ 29. I am a very precise communicator.

> _____ 30. I can sit with another person, not say anything, and still be comfortable.
> _____ 31. I think that untalkative people are boring.
> _____ 32. I am an extremely open communicator.
>
> Scoring: Reverse your score for Items 4, 6, 7, 10, 16, 19, 21, 22, 23, 24, 25, 28, 29, 31, and 32. If your original score was 1, reverse it to a 9; if your original score was a 2, reverse it to an 8; and so on. After reversing the score for those 15 items, simply sum the 32 items. Lower scores indicate low-context communication. Higher scores indicate high-context communication.
>
> (Gudykunst et al., 1996)

Developing Contextual and Critical Consciousness Using Reflective Questions

As discussed in earlier parts of this book, critical consciousness is our ability to recognize oppressive social forces and to make conscious efforts to challenge those forces (Garcia et al., 2009). What this means is that when someone becomes critically conscious or aware, they use their evolving understanding of and their ability to relate personally to oppressive societal discourses, and work or take actions to influence or change them. What this means in our training and development as therapists is that we continuously work to minimize oppressive experiences in therapy for our clients by examining personal biases. The following questions can help us to examine our own development of critical consciousness. And as you will see, depending on how you identify, you may need to challenge yourself to consider other identities not mentioned in this set of questions. They are just a starting point for your personal reflection. The following questions were adapted and are used with permission from the first author (Garcia et al., 2009, p. 38).

Exploring Therapist Privilege

1. In what ways have my or my ancestors' accomplishments benefited others and/or been at others' expense?
2. In what ways have my ancestors used race, economics, gender, and politics to foster both past and present day disparities?

Exploring Therapist Responsibility

1. In what ways do I fulfill my moral obligation to correct current social inequities? Are these ways meaningful to those who have been wronged or just meaningful to me?
2. What do I do in clinical work, on a day-to-day basis, that might contribute to the structuring of unequal outcomes?

Exploring Therapist Attitudes and Biases

1. How do I demonstrate callousness either overtly (e.g., demanding that those without boots or straps pull themselves up by their bootstraps) or covertly (e.g., championing more materials for "gifted" students while ignoring the needs of students who lag behind)?
2. What are my feelings during an interaction with a person from a working/upper-class background? How does that interaction affect how I feel about myself? If such feelings were elicited by a working/upper-class client, how might my work be affected?
3. What are my "family values," and how inclusive are they of gays, lesbians, bisexuals, and transgender people and their families?
4. Do I, as therapist, accept that a healthy, happy, and "normal" life is compatible with being gay or lesbian?
5. Would I be willing to be a client of a gay or lesbian therapist/supervisor?

Exploring the Process of Critical Consciousness Socialization

1. In what ways do my reactions of fear, avoidance, and devaluation of this process derail my progress towards socializing my critical consciousness?
2. In what ways do my colleagues and/or supervisors, provide me adequate support and challenge me to deepen commitment to socializing my critical consciousness?
3. What is my investment in my understanding of how to be an antiracist clinician?
4. What self-image do I have as a result of my good intentions towards racially marginalized clients?

Exploring Therapist Views of Client Behavior

1. What part of the behavior of clients may be interpreted as resistance to further marginalization?

2. What clinical choices might I make differently if I were to view some of the "presenting" behavior as positive—as opposition or challenge to further disempowerment—instead of viewing it as antisocial acting out?
3. How are we "empowered" and "disempowered" in our work and development as therapists? What and how are we resisting?

Summary

This chapter served as an invitation to deepen your personal understanding of your own multifaceted sociocultural identity. We also hope that you spent time in reflection about the impact of oppressive forces in your own life and in the lives of others you are connected to. Our vision for the activities from this chapter, is that after you have spent time progressing through many of the exercises and activities and working through your own thoughts and feelings related to the topics that you would take the next step to share your process with others. We believe with our whole hearts, and from our own experiences, that participating in critically conscious and growth supporting conversations with others can only enrich your life and your work as a clinician.

Note

1 Adapted from Bernstein (2000); Burton et al. (2004); Heron (2005); Killian (2001); Kondrat (1999).

References

Arvin, M., Tuck, E., & Morrill, A. (2013). Decolonizing feminism: Challenging connections between settler colonialism and heteropatriarchy. *Feminist Formations*, 25(1), 8–34.
Bem, S. L. (1981). Gender schema theory: A cognitive account of sex typing. *Psychological Review*, 88(4), 354–364.
Bernstein, A. (2000). Straight therapists working with lesbians and gays in family therapy. *Journal of Marital & Family Therapy*, 26, 443–454.
Bronfenbrenner, U. (1979). *The ecology of human development: Experiments by nature and design*. Cambridge, MA: Harvard University Press.
Burton, L. M., Winn, D.-M., Stevenson, H., & Clark, S. L. (2004). Working with African American clients: Considering the "homeplace" in marriage and family therapy practices. *Journal of Marital & Family Therapy*, 30, 397–410.
Cass, V. C. (1979). Homosexual identity formation: A theoretical model. *Journal of Homosexuality*, 4(3), 219–235.
Cross, W. E., Jr. (1971). The Negro-to-Black conversion experience: Toward a psychology of Black liberation. *Black World*, 20, 13–27.

David, E. J. R., & Okazaki, S. (2006). Colonial mentality: A review and recommendation for Filipino American psychology. *Cultural Diversity and Ethnic Minority Psychology, 12*(1), 1–16.

Dunbar-Ortiz, R. (2014). *An indigenous peoples' history of the United States*. Boston, MA: Beacon Press.

Erikson, E. (1968). *Identity: Youth and crisis*. New York: Norton.

Garcia, M., Kosutic, I., McDowell, T., & Anderson, S. A. (2009). Raising critical consciousness in family therapy supervision. *Journal of Feminist Family Therapy, 21*, 18–38.

Gergen, K. (2009). An invitation to social construction. *Social construction: Revolution in the making*. Thousand Oaks, CA: Sage, 1–13.

Greenwald, A. G., & Banaji, M. R. (1995). Implicit social cognition: Attitudes, self-esteem, and stereotypes. *Psychological Review, 102*(1), 4–27.

Gudykunst, W. B., Matsumoto, Y., Ting-Toomey, S., Nishida, T., Kim, K., & Heyman, S. (1996). The influence of cultural individualism: Collectivism, self construals, and individual values on communication styles across cultures. *Human Communication Research, 22*(4), 510–543.

Hardy, K. V., & Laszloffy, T. A. (1995). The cultural genogram: Key to training culturally competent family therapists. *Journal of Marital and Family Therapy, 21*(3), 227–237.

Hardy, K. V., & Laszloffy, T. A. (2008). The dynamics of a pro-racist ideology: Implications for family therapists. In M. McGoldrick & K. V. Hardy (Eds.), *Re-Visioning family therapy: Race cultures, and gender in clinical practice* (2nd ed.) (pp. 225–237). New York, NY: Guilford.

Hays, P. (2008). *Addressing cultural competencies in practice: Assessment, diagnosis and therapy* (2nd ed.). Washington, DC: American Psychological Association.

Heinze, P. (2008). Let's talk about race, baby. *Multicultural Education, 16*(Fall), 2–11.

Helms, J. E. (1995). I also said: "White racial identity influences white researchers.". *The Counseling Psychologist, 21*(2), 240–243.

Heron, B. (2005). Self-reflection in critical social work practice: Subjectivity and the possibilities of resistance. *Reflective Practice, 6*(3), 341–351.

Keiley, M. K., Dolbin, M., Hill, J., Karuppaswamy, N., Liu, T., Natrajan, R., ... Robinson, P. (2002). The cultural genogram: Experiences from a within a marriage and family therapy training program. *Journal of Marital and Family Therapy, 28*(2), 165–178.

Killian, K. (2001). Reconstructing racial histories and identities: The narratives of interracial couples. *Journal of Marital & Family Therapy, 27*(1), 27–42.

Kondrat, M. E. (1999). Who is the "self" in self-aware: Professional self-awareness from a critical theory perspective. *Social Service Review, 73*, 451–477.

Kosutic, I., Garcia, M., Graves, T., Barnett, F., Hall, J., Haley, E., ... Kaiser, B. (2009). The critical genogram: A tool for promoting critical consciousness. *Journal of Feminist Family Therapy, 21*, 151–176.

McGeorge, C., & Carlson, T. S. (2011). Deconstructing heterosexism: Becoming an LGB affirmative herterosexual couple and family therapist. *Journal of Marital and Family Therapy, 37*(1), 14–26.

McGoldrick, M., Gerson, R., & Petry, S. (2008). *Genograms: Assessment and intervention* (3rd ed.). New York: Norton.

McGoldrick, M., Pearce, J., & Giordano, J. (Eds.) (2005). *Ethnicity and family therapy* (3rd ed.). New York: Guilford.

Mittal, M., & Wieling, E. (2006). Training experiences of international students in marriage and family therapy. *Journal of Marital and Family Therapy, 32*(2), 369–383.

Neuliep, J. W. (2012). *Intercultural communication: A contextual approach*. Thousand Oaks, CA: SAGE Publications.

Phinney, J. S. (1989). Stages of ethnic identity development in minority group adolescents. *The Journal of Early Adolescence, 9*, 34–49.

Piaget, J., & Cook, M. T. (1952). *The origins of intelligence in children*. New York: International University Press.

Robinson-Wood, T. (2017). *The convergence of race, ethnicity, and gender: Multiple identities in counseling* (5th ed.). Thousand Oaks, CA: Sage.

Rock, M., Carlson, T. S., & McGeorge, C. R. (2010). Does affirmative training matter? Assessing CFT students' beliefs about sexual orientation and their level of affirmative training. *Journal of Marital and Family Therapy, 36*(2), 171–184.

Root, M. P. P. (2003). Racial identity development and persons of mixed-race heritage. In M. P. P. Root & M. Kelly (Eds.), *The multiracial child resource book: Living complex identities* (pp. 34–41). Seattle, WA: Mavin Foundation.

Shin, R. Q. (2015). The application of critical consciousness and intersectionality as tools for decolonizing racial/ethnic identity development models in the fields of counseling and psychology. In R. D. Goodman & P. C. Gorski (Eds.), *Decolonizing "multicultural" counseling through social justice* (pp. 11–22). New York: Springer-Verlag, International and Cultural Psychology, doi: 10.1007/978-1-4939-1283-4_2.

Sorrells, K. (2016). *Intercultural communication: Globalization and social justice* (2nd ed.). Thousand Oaks, CA: Sage.

Tajfel, H. (1974). Social identity and intergroup behavior. *Social Science Information, 13*(2), 65–93.

Tatum, B. D. (1997). *"Why are all the black kids sitting together in the cafeteria?" and other conversations about race*. New York: Basic Books.

Thomas, A. J., & Schwarzbaum, S. E. (2017). *Culture and identity: Life stories for counselors and therapists*. Thousand Oaks, CA: Sage.

University of Michigan. (2017, August 16). The spectrum activity: Questions of identity. Spectrum center and the program on intergroup relations, LSA inclusive teaching initiative [Online content]. Retrieved from https://sites.lsa.umich.edu/inclusive-teaching/2017/08/16/1213/#more-1213.

Wieling, E., & Rastogi, M. (2003). Voices of marriage and family therapists of color: An exploratory survey. *Journal of Feminist Family Therapy, 15*(1), 1–18.

Wijeyesinghe, C. L. (2012). The intersectional model of multiracial identity. In C. L. Wijeyesinghe & B. W. Jackson III (Eds.), *New perspectives on racial identity development: Integrating and emerging frameworks* (2nd ed.). New York: New York University Press.

Wilkins, E. J., Whiting, J. B., Watson, M. F., Russon, J. M., & Moncrief, A. M. (2013). Residual effects of slavery: What clinicians need to know. *Contemporary Family Therapy: An International Journal, 35*(1), 14–28.

Worthington, R. L., & Mohr, J. J. (2002). Theorizing heterosexual identity development. *The Counseling Psychologist, 30*, 491–495.

Moving Toward Sociocultural Relational Connection

7

From the time that we first thought of this book until now, much has shifted in our socio-political context that can make it even more difficult to communicate around challenging topics. Many of us were not raised in families that modeled well-differentiated, responsive conversations related to identity, socio-contextual topics, and issues of power in relationships. Most certainly, this is not modeled for us in the political arena. What we internalize from political discourse is that there are certain sides and beliefs that are bad and wrong and we need to do what we can to stay with the right side. If not, we will most likely be shamed, attacked, or seen as incompetent. Witnessing people get attacked and shamed in the public sphere, let alone in our own families, is traumatizing and shuts down our own abilities to keep an open mind and open heart to such dialogue.

In Chapter 6, we offered what we hope are helpful ways that all of us, whether beginning therapists in training or advanced clinicians, can engage in personal growth and self-of-the-therapist development. In this chapter, we will discuss the possible reasons, from MFT theories and literature, for barriers and challenges in sociocontextual dialogue. We will offer a framework for the stages of sociocultural relational connection. Then we will more specifically address how to move toward and bring these topics to the forefront of relationships, considering our self-identity, dyadic relationships, group contexts, and institutional dynamics.

Why there are Barriers and Challenges from an MFT Perspective

Our field has many excellent theories that illuminate why there are challenges to interpersonal communication and connection in sociocontexual conversations. We want to highlight a few theories and concepts that could help us better understand ourselves and those with whom we wish to have more authentic connection.

Bowenian Family Systems Theory

Bowenian Family Systems Theory (BFST) is a foundational theory in the field of MFT. According to founder Murray Bowen, relational problems are connected to our level of reactivity and anxiety. One of his hallmark concepts, differentiation of self, is "an individual's ability to separate [their] instinctually driven emotional reaction from [their] thoughtfully considered goal-directed functioning" (Titelman, 1998, p. 14). When we have higher levels of differentiation, we can be autonomous and individuated while remaining interconnected with others. (Note: In a more comprehensive discussion about BFST, we would decenter the Western White patriarchal assumptions about what is considered "well-differentiated" and what is considered enmeshed.)

Individual level of differentiation is shaped by our families-of-origin and the multi-generational transfer of chronic anxiety. If we grew up in a context where it was not permissible to have differences of opinion (low differentiation and high anxiety) then it is harder to engage in conversations related to difference, unless we have engaged in thoughtful reflection and interpersonal work. We might shy away from difficult conversations because that was what was modeled for us, or we might experience intense anxiety thinking that a difference of perspective means we are being attacked. In any case, it is important to understand our family contexts as they interrelate to our desire to move toward communicating about challenging topics.

Contextual Differentiation

This is a term that I (Jessica) thought of while I was teaching at California State University, Northridge (ChenFeng, 2018). When I studied my own clinical processes in private practice working with a predominantly Asian American second-generation population, I found that much of the clinical work revolved around increasing differentiation at the sociocultural and contextual levels. If we understand individual differentiation to be the ability to identify one's own thoughts and feelings separate from that of the family, then contextual differentiation is identifying one's own thoughts and feelings as they are influenced by, related to, or different from one's context.

If we take this concept and consider our own contextual differentiation, most of us typically have a lower level because we are not raised or socialized to consider how the larger context shapes our identity and being. As an Asian American woman, if I am not aware of how the model minority stereotype and White heteropatriarchy impacts my sense of self, I might have a harder time identifying experiences of sexism or even sexual harassment from older White male colleagues because of the unconscious ways that I feel pressured to live up to model minority ideas (i.e. being compliant, expected to maintain peace, social propriety).

Narrative Therapy

Narrative Therapy is one of our postmodern theories, founded by Michael White. He talked about how cultural stories determine the shape of our individual life narratives.

> People make sense of their lives through stories, both the cultural narratives they are born into and the personal narratives they construct in relation to the cultural narratives. In any culture, certain narratives will come to be dominant over other narratives. These dominant narratives will specify the preferred and customary ways of believing and behaving within the particular culture. Some cultures have colonized and oppressed others. The narratives of the dominant culture are then imposed on people of marginalized cultures.
> (Freedman & Combs, 1996, p. 32)

The presence of dominant narratives makes it difficult for us to consider possibilities outside of, or different from those narratives. Dominant narratives regarding the way things should be, what is right, what or who is better, can sometimes be so fixed in people's beliefs that within relationships, it is nearly impossible to have room for another perspective. We hope that you have been observing and deconstructing some of the dominant narratives in your context so that you can have space to hold the alternative narratives of those with whom you seek connection.

Building Clinical Courage

As we grow in our ability and capacity to engage in difficult conversations, we are building clinical skills for better serving clients. Much of this growth and interpersonal work is about moving toward tolerating and embracing tension, and being okay with sitting in our own not-knowingness. This builds our clinical courage, allowing us to feel more and more secure in our ability to work with a diverse clinical population because we better know and understand ourselves.

As we work on our own differentiation and deconstruct gripping dominant narratives, we can have fewer experiences of reacting out of anxiety or judging (i.e. getting upset with a client, telling a client what to do instead of remaining curious, mind blanking or feeling stuck, correcting). We can hold an open posture to truly hear and know the other, whether it is a client, colleague, or friend.

Stages of Sociocultural Relational Connection

While conducting research for this book, we did not come across any theories or frameworks that provided what we were looking for in terms of describing the progression of relationships as they move toward more authentic connection around sociocultural issues. So, we came up with our own!

We are calling this framework the *Stages of Sociocultural Relational Connection*. These stages describe relationships where the raising of critical consciousness becomes mutual and intentional. There are five stages that move along a general continuum with increasing levels of five attributes. These attributes are: civility, sociocultural interest, personal sociocultural awareness, relational sociocultural curiosity, and attunement to relational power (Table 7.1).

Stage One: Civility and Trust

Moving toward authentic connection around sociocultural issues requires a baseline level of civility and capacity for trust building. The nuts and bolts of creating relational civility and trust are beyond the scope of this book, but we want to share what we are thinking in regard to these ideas. We appreciate the definition of civility by the Institute for Civility in Government:

> Civility is about more than just politeness, although politeness is a necessary first step. It is about disagreeing without disrespect, seeking common ground as a starting point for dialogue about differences, listening past one's preconceptions, and teaching others to do the same. Civility is the hard work of staying present even with those with whom we have deep-rooted and fierce disagreement.
>
> (ICG website)

The concept of civility is complex. It may be perceived as a tool to silence anger, or to make White people (or other dominant group person) feel less uncomfortable. That is not what we mean by civility. We see it as something that begins in us—a positioning of our selves such that we are open to being pleasantly surprised by the other. It is interlaced with the open heart, open mind, and open hand posture. As relationships move through these five stages, civility grows.

Stage one is when two colleagues are in relationship but things stay at a socially appropriate, politically correct place. There is a baseline level of politeness and civility, though they have not yet broached any topics related to social location or sociocultural issues. It is not clear if the colleague is interested in sociocultural issues. They might enjoy their relationship—it is collegial, friendly, fun, and they work well together. Or perhaps they do not know each other well quite yet and things are cordial and warm. It seems that many work relationships stay in this arena. In this stage, people are not interested in or comfortable with moving toward dialogue that involves sociocultural issues. In supervision or in class, interactions and exchanges are essentially about clinical work with clients. Theories are discussed, interventions role-played, but there is no integration of sociocultural issues regarding clients or therapists. In clinics or in academic programs that do not address issues of diversity and equity, this is not uncommon.

Stage Two: Sociocultural Interest

The second stage moves one step toward sociocultural openness and connection through the presence of sociocultural interest. Two people in a working relationship begin to make comments about, refer to, or bring up topics related to sociocultural context. This might involve having conversations about politics, a recent election, or the latest sitcom. A stage two supervisory relationship would integrate issues of sociocultural context into clinical work at a basic level of understanding. Conversations about clients' social location might not reflect an intersectional perspective, focusing on a few parts of identity (race or religion) in a static way. Diversity issues are important to the supervisor or in the academic context, but from a distance. They are relevant to clinical work in the way that it helps for understanding difference, but there is no understanding about equity and the structural issues of power.

Sociocultural interest can be anything from talking about race or religion as it relates to a recent movie, or expressing interest in issues of gender bias in the workplace. Sociocultural interest might start off peripherally and unintentionally and move toward more thoughtful intentional engagement. This attribute is simply interest in the issues themselves, and not necessarily attached or connected to relationship (as the next two attributes will be). This is one of the first indicators that a relationship can begin to move toward a sociocultural relational connection. There is further development of civility and trust because it seems important to the colleague that such topics have value.

Stage Three: Relational Sociocultural Curiosity

Sociocultural interest expands to a relational sociocultural curiosity—not only caring about particular topics, but about people themselves. Someone who used to only focus on racial issues might now expand their curiosity to include other social location identifiers, particularly those important to their colleague. Two people in relationship might begin to wonder about one another, starting with curiosities such as "What is it like to be one of the only _____ in our MFT program?" or being curious about a classmate or supervisee's immigration story or ancestry. This is stage three, where two people are talking about the experiences of one another, whether this is between supervisor and supervisee(s) or also with clients. In supervision, the supervisor expresses interest in the supervisee's social location. Or the therapist is encouraged by the supervisor to be more curious about the client's social location. There may be a basic level of understanding that it matters to the other person to talk about these areas and so with good intention, there is a move toward relational sociocultural curiosity. There is a deepening of civility and trust because each person may feel a little more seen and heard because a colleague is curious about who they are.

Stage Four: Personal Sociocultural Awareness

A relationship that moves to stage four makes a significant shift. Individuals begin to consider how the self is a part of sociocultural realities and dynamics. Personal sociocultural awareness involves an individual being cognizant of their own sociocultural identity. It is important to be curious about the other, but exploring more about oneself has significant impact on the relationship. In self-reflection, the individual might ask: How connected am I to the various parts of my own social location such as through the ADDRESSING framework? As I go about my day, how aware am I of my social location as I navigate relationships and various spaces? When we first start to develop critical consciousness, we may be more conscious of how society engages with certain parts of our social location (e.g. our experiences with our racial or gender identity). As we delve deeper, we expand our awareness such as engaging with the exercises in Chapter 6. Doing our own self-work allows for our relationships to grow to this stage and beyond.

Bringing personal awareness into the relationship transforms how we are curious about the other person. The curiosity is less of a simple wondering, and becomes more a curiosity of care, concern, and empathy. An individual might think to themselves: "In my own self-discovery, I realized that sometimes I feel silenced as a woman of color. I wonder if my other classmates feel this way too regarding their social location." Social location is less of a topic or issue, but more about who people are and how we relate. The increase in mutual investment with one another builds the trust further.

In supervision, supervisors or supervisees become more acutely aware of their identities and how they interact with others. Therapists start to use their personal sociocultural awareness as part of their treatment planning and interventions. They recognize that their social location impacts clients.

Stage Five: Attunement to Relational Power

When we reach stage five, a relationship is ready for continued growth because of the attunement to relational power. This is similar to the idea of content vs. process. It is a bit easier to talk about the "content"—our racial identities, our religious backgrounds—but it is not so easy to talk about process of how these impact and shape our actual relationship with one another. It is the willingness to continue to look at how power dynamics in the relationship shift and play out in various contexts. It moves the personal sociocultural awareness from "If I'm having this experience, maybe my classmates are too" to "I tend to feel anxious in this class and I wonder if it's because of internalized racism that gets activated in the class discussions?" It is possible that when we attune to the power in a relationship, we recognize that it may not have the trust-building capacity we hoped for. The other party, or we ourselves, may need to do more self-work before the relationship can grow in a way that is mutually supportive.

With attunement to relational power, a supervisor's personal awareness of their power would compel them to check in with supervisees about their dynamic and to ask for feedback. In the clinical setting, a therapist may become aware of the discomfort they feel as it relates to the power differential with the client and talk to their supervisor about it. Between classmates, one person may want to check in with another about how having more relational power impacts the way they talk about certain topics or the dynamics of the supervision group.

Table 7.1 Stages of Sociocultural Relational Connection

	Stage 1	Stage 2	Stage 3	Stage 4	Stage 5
Civility and Trust			Increases across stages		
Sociocultural Interest					
Relational Curiosity					
Personal Sociocultural Awareness					
Attunement to Relational Power					

Note: Shaded areas represent when the five attributes are present across the five stages.

How to Use the Stages of Sociocultural Relational Connection

Having this model allows us to reflect on what stage of sociocultural relational connection we are in with a colleague. It is not meant to be prescriptive or to describe every relationship progression. It offers general principles for how each stage might look, but every dyadic connection is different for many reasons.

If we have a general sense that we might be at stage two with a colleague and understand what stage three might look like, we can ask ourselves whether this is a relationship we want to and can move to the next stage. Below are examples of catalyzing questions or statements that could shift a relationship from one stage to the next. We are assuming that you, the user of these questions/statements, has sociocultural interest, relational curiosity, are open to personal sociocultural awareness, and also want to grow in attunement to relational power.

Helpful Questions/Statements According to Stage of Sociocultural Relational Connection

Stage One to Two: Civility and Trust to Sociocultural Interest

- What did you think of the movie *Crazy Rich Asians*? It's supposed to be a big deal in Hollywood with that much Asian American representation in one movie.
- The situation with building the border wall has gotten so out of hand. What does your community think about it?
- I just heard that Nike has a campaign highlighting Colin Kaepernick. That's a pretty big move for a company like Nike huh?
- Can I ask for your thoughts? My daughter came home from school with a children's book about having two moms. I'm not quite sure how to talk to her about it.
- I've heard you talk about _____ and I'd like to learn more about it. Would it be possible to incorporate discussions about _____ into our supervision process?

Stage Two to Three: Sociocultural Interest to Relational Curiosity

- You mentioned that you grew up in Taiwan and came here for college. What has that experience been like for you?
- Thanks for sharing more about your experience as a Muslim American and wearing a hijab. Would you be open to talking about what that's like when you do therapy with clients?
- I'm sorry that I don't have much personal experience with family or friends who have visual impairment. Do you feel like you have the support you need from us as classmates?

Stage Three to Four: Relational Curiosity to Personal Awareness

- In other spaces in my life, I feel like I can talk about my experience as a first-generation graduate student and having impostor syndrome. Is that something I can be more open about with you?
- The #metoo movement has really impacted me and I think it's seeping through in my work with male clients. Can you support me in talking through this?
- I'm just starting to understand the privilege that comes with my having U.S. citizenship. I'm working on being more sensitive to clients who may be undocumented and exploring their experiences.
- I hope this is okay to ask you about. I've been more aware of my own experiences as a woman of color so I'm curious how it is for you being the only female faculty of color in our program?
- Wow I'm sorry that I never learned about colonization and what indigenous people have gone through. I want to take the time to learn about whose land I am on.

Stage Four to Five: Personal Awareness to Attunement to Relational Power

- Thanks for your patience with me. I just recently learned about gender pronouns and I want to keep working at using the pronouns that respect you and others.

- I recognize that I'm a generation older than you and it might be hard culturally for you to tell me what you're really thinking about our project. Can I check in with you about that?
- I think I might have just mansplained, but I'm not sure. Would you be willing to give me feedback about it?

As we seek to grow and develop more authentic relationships, there is a natural ebb and flow from feeling more connected to possibly experiencing relational ruptures. We all make unintentional mistakes that hurt others, ourselves, and the relationship. These are opportunities for growth and connection. Here are some post-rupture questions for reflection, whether we have or do not have relational power in a relationship, whether we feel harmed or have caused harm to another.

Post-Rupture Questions for Reflection

- What feelings come up for me and how are they connected to my social location (in my privilege and/or in my marginalized identity)?
- If I feel tension, what might the tension be about?
- What is it about my position/relational power that contributes to this dynamic?
- What might the other person be feeling?
- What dominant discourses fuel this dynamic? How might I actively work to deconstruct these?
- What alternative discourses would facilitate relational connection?
- If this rupture goes unaddressed, what are the personal risks and benefits? Relational risks and benefits?
- If I address this rupture, what are the personal risks and benefits? Relational risks and benefits?

There is one last piece we would like to address which is the responsibility we have in evaluating the context for whether a relationship can move to the next stage, or if processing a rupture is worthwhile. It is not wise to attempt connection and move toward vulnerability with anyone and everyone. There is always the possibility of harm and even trauma. There are issues beyond the scope of this book to consider: the mental health/well-being of ourselves and others and personality issues that impact connection. There are always benefits and risks to relationship growth and we encourage you to review our discussion related to this in Chapter 1.

Summary

Our hope is that this chapter offers a way to think about moving toward more authentic connection in your professional and personal world. It takes courage to be open to each next stage in the Stages of Sociocultural Relational Connection. The questions and reflections offered here are meant to support you in developing such relationships in the field and to create spaces for you to be seen and heard as a whole intersectional person. We welcome your feedback on how this framework translates to your experiences. In the next and last chapter, we send you off with words of wisdom and support from our dear colleagues and friends in the field.

Questions for Reflection

1. In what stage in the Stages of Sociocultural Relational Connection do you find yourself in your own relationships?
2. Is there someone in your life that you want to grow in connection with? What stage is your relationship in? What might it look like for it to move toward the next stage? What would you need in order for this to be a possibility?
3. Are there relationships in your life that are at stage five? If so, what did it take for the relationship to develop in that way? What was your role in that development? What was the role of the other person? How do you maintain continued support, connection, and accountability in that relationship?

References

ChenFeng, J. (2018). Integration of self and family: Asian American Christians in the midst of White Evangelicalism and being the model minority. In E. Esmiol & L. Nice (Eds.), *Socially just religious and spiritual interventions: Ethical uses of therapeutic power* (pp. 15–26). Switzerland: Springer.

Freedman, J., & Combs, G. (1996). *Narrative therapy: The social construction of preferred realities*. New York: Norton.

Titelman, P. (1998). Overview of the Bowen theoretical-therapeutic system. In P. Titelman (Ed.), *Clinical applications of Bowen family systems theory* (pp. 7–50). Philadelphia, PA: The Haworth Press.

8

Establishing a Foundation for a Career of Being Known and Knowing Others

In this final chapter of the book, we would like to offer you one more cornerstone for establishing a meaningful and flourishing career and identity as an MFT: a community of support. This is a critical component of our clinical development. It is the intra and interpersonal relationships that allow us to remain authentic, that empower us, and that support our continued growth of critical consciousness and self-reflexivity that will sustain us throughout a career. First we will talk about what active engagement in creating a support system might look like as it relates to a career in the field. Then we talk about establishing and maintaining relationships with intention. In this chapter we will also share other voices from the field of MFT, our own colleagues and friends who have helped us and continue to support us on our lifelong journey to remain culturally humble and accountable to our own growth and to the growth of others (colleagues, supervisees, and clients). Finally, in this chapter we will offer some recommendations and resources for moving forward on the journey.

Preparing a Support System

In our journey from pre-licensed to licensed MFT we have both found it so important to intentionally develop a support system along the way. Of course while you are in graduate school and while you are earning your hours toward licensure, you need the support of professors, supervisors, and colleagues, loved ones and friends. But what we mean to focus on here is that extra level of support to empower you to find and maintain your voice in these multiple contexts. This journey of bringing your whole self into your work as a therapist requires trusted colleagues or partners on the journey with whom you may share feelings, attitudes, and decisions connected to your process and experiences. It also means constructing and reconstructing relationships with important others in your life outside of the field such as: friends, family (family of origin and chosen family), partners or spouses, and your children.

First, we want to speak a bit to the process of changing support systems as a result of entering the field of family therapy. Many students have shared with us how their interpersonal relationships shift throughout their time in graduate school. Sometimes this is because of our own education and first time learning about systems theories, diagnoses/assessments —and it is expected that we would reflect on our own families and relationships as we are integrating new knowledge into our realities. Other times, friends and family start to interact with us as though we might be their therapist, asking for advice, consulting with us or shifting the relationship's expectations. These types of changes can be disorienting—we may not know how to respond, how to set up boundaries and maintain connection at the same time. Oftentimes these might be relationships we have had for many years and we may not have had to develop new or different support systems. In my first year of teaching MFT students, my (Jessica) students asked about this process of shifting relational connections and support systems. I shared about my own way of conceptualizing support systems and when I drew this on the board, students expressed that it was a helpful diagram. We want to share it with you here.

Relational Support Diagram

I (Jessica) am using myself as an example in this Relational Support Diagram (Figure 8.1). There are a few parts of myself that I find valuable and necessary to be connected to: faith/spirituality, Asian American identity and experiences, clinical/therapist experiences, and academic/scholarly interests (I will call these spheres). In this diagram, I am represented by the small, light grey circle. The other black circles are people with whom I can connect around these four parts of my life. I may have grown up with friends at church with whom I feel connection around our shared spirituality or other Asian American friends where in the relationship we

[Diagram: Jessica's Relational Support Diagram with four overlapping spheres labeled "Faith + Spirituality," "Asian American Identity + Experiences," "Clinical + Therapist Experiences," and "Academic + Scholarly Interests," with "SELF" at the center and dots representing people placed within and across the spheres.]

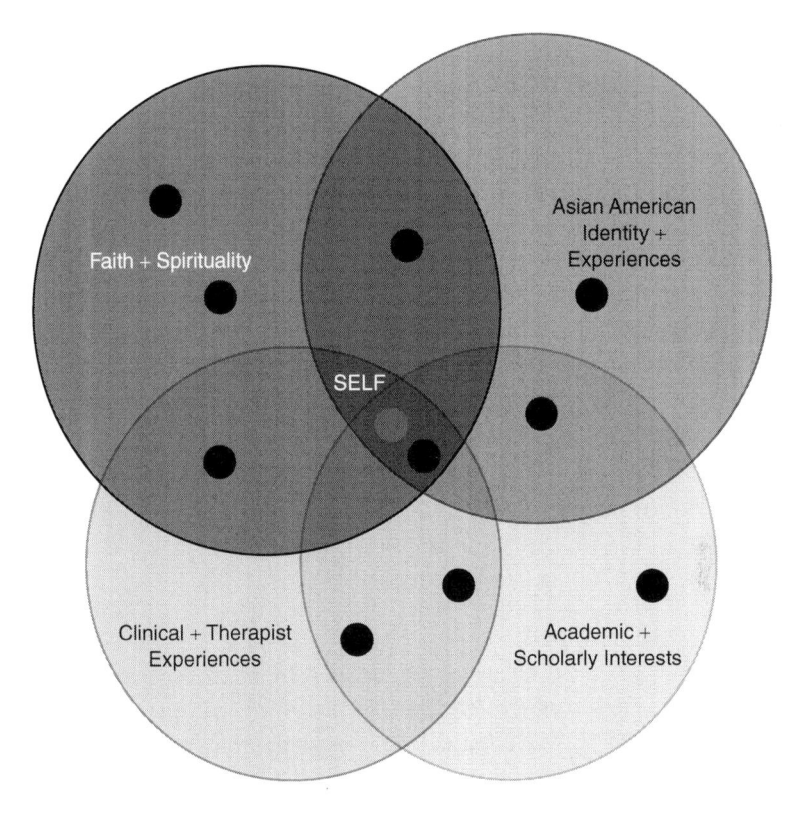

Figure 8.1 Jessica's example of a Relational Support Diagram

connect around our racial experiences or cultural backgrounds. Sometimes these spheres overlap: I have an Asian American colleague who is also working on her PhD so we can engage around cultural/racial experiences as they intersect with research and the academic community. As you can see from the diagram, there are different people in these four spheres—with some people intersecting across one or more of these areas.

Each of us has a different number of spheres; the spheres may have different size/weight through different seasons of our lives. They can also come and go through these seasons. Different people may move between the various spaces of the spheres. For some of us, it may be rare to have even one person who occupies all the spheres, someone with whom we feel our most integrated authentic self. Our encouragement is that as our identities are so complex and multifaceted, the expectation is not necessarily that we have everyone we care about occupying all the spheres, but rather that it is normal to have different parts of ourselves attended to at different times and with different people.

We believe that becoming a marriage and family therapist catalyzes a major shift in our lives—a shift that is not only cognitive but also intrapersonal and interpersonal. Just as much as our identities are evolving, so are our relationships and support systems, personally and professionally. In this chapter, we call on colleagues from the field to share the ways they remain engaged and committed to their own growth and development as well as grounded and connected to each other on their career journeys. Here we have just a few tips and suggestions for building your supportive community now and the ways you can actively maintain them as you move forward, and in some cases away from your safety net!

Building Relationships with Intention

Earlier in this book we talked about the benefit of mentors and support groups. Researchers have found that, especially for students who identify with marginalized or underrepresented identities, having a structure in place to check-in and process experiences on the educational and training journey is crucial for longevity. Oftentimes these groupings form naturally in your cohort, in your graduate program, or with others from your field site. If you are early in your graduate program and have not found a niche, we encourage you to reach out to people around you. If someone from one of your classes says something that strikes you, tell them. If someone else says they are not sure where to go for the best coffee or to study, suggest you figure it out together. Other ways to make connections on a larger scale would be to create a phone tree with members of your cohort or a social media private group page where your peers and colleagues can connect outside of class to share ideas, resources, or to make plans for future gatherings or events.

It may also be helpful to create a sense of community with individuals with whom you feel a sense of connection for reasons that may not be academic or supervisory. Many of us need connection with people who "look" like us (e.g. race or gender), share a similar identity status (e.g. sexual orientation), or who share similar values or beliefs as us (e.g. faith or religion or political views). For example, in the Black community with everything that is going on socially and politically known to be threatening and harmful on a daily basis, creating space for accountability, checking-in, and extra support is one way to maintain resilience (Wilkins et al., 2013). Within your program you may find that you are only one of a few Black women or one of a few males, or one of the only Deaf students. You may be able to find other students with whom to build a community from within the program, but if not, we want to encourage you to look outside students in your cohort or program. You may consider talking to a faculty member who can offer you support and a sense of connection. From my experience as one of the only faculty of color, I (Dana) noticed that students were seeking me out for discussions and support beyond supervision or class content. I have now made it clear that I am available for check-ins with students. Another thing to consider would be programs on campus that have created spaces and the sense of community you might need. Oftentimes graduate students forget that they have access to the larger college or university student organizations and support networks. I always try to tell my students about these resources early in the program, but starting graduate school can be overwhelming, so personal resources may not be remembered.

If you have been fortunate enough to form meaningful relationships with members of your cohort, colleagues at your field site, or elsewhere in the field (at conferences or workshops, networking events, etc.), we encourage you to make the concerted effort to keep connections and relationships going beyond school and practicum. We have both found that the relationships you make while in graduate school and at your training sites can be a life force on your journey as an MFT. Both of us have continued to maintain our relationships with those people who have made such a difference in our professional lives and development in numerous ways. First, we meet up with colleagues at conferences locally and nationally. We make time to talk, catch up, and spend time together refueling. We work on projects with colleagues in person and virtually. Virtual connections such as FaceTime and Skype/Zoom have been critical for both of us in maintaining our relationship to each other and to each of our trusted colleagues and friends in the field. It gives us the sense of "seeing" and working with people who look like us or share our values and passion for the work we do on a more regular basis. Time and distance can be prohibitive, however, with a little effort, those barriers can be overcome. Some suggestions for how to really make it work include: taking the initiative even if you are an introvert; scheduling the next FaceTime during the current meeting; and staying connected in between with a group email or text chain. These things may seem arbitrary now, as you are reading, but it is so easy to lose a connection because of the busyness of our schedules. A simple group text to share some struggle or good news can really make the difference for everyone.

Stories from the Field

As mentioned at the start of this chapter, we thought it would be helpful to ask our esteemed colleagues who are and have been committed to bringing their whole selves to their clinical work, in order to enrich your perspective and open up the possibilities for how you can keep this going through your schooling, your post graduate training, and into licensure. Both of us have consciously nurtured the impactful and meaningful relationships with our colleagues from our graduate programs, clinical training, and leadership positions, and we have made conscious efforts to cultivate new relationships in our teaching and work environments. In this section we will first introduce you to our colleagues and then we will share their responses to three specific questions.

José

I (Jessica) met José the year that the Liberation Based Healing Conference (LBHC) was held at California State University, Northridge (CSUN). He was a CSUN faculty member in the social work department and also coordinating the conference. I volunteered to help and so we got to know each other in a conference-planning context. José is such a wealth of knowledge and is the person who really shaped my understanding of settler colonialism and the experience of Indigenous peoples. He also teaches and shares from a position of humility and kindness. As we have taught for one another's classes, I have seen how he models having an open heart and spirit so that students remain engaged and curious. We have been able to be resources to one another and for each other's students. It is such an amazing feeling to direct a student to your colleague (for mentorship around sociocultural issues) and completely trust that the student is in good hands. That is how I feel with José.

I (Dana) was privileged and honored to be introduced to José by Jessica! What a gift his presence has been in my work life. We started off getting to know each other in conversation with Jessica—and because of the nature and context of their relationship, there was space in our relationship to talk about power and privilege, race, gender ... everything. And it was José who helped me to integrate acknowledgement and more critical consideration of the experiences of Indigenous peoples into my consciousness. I am constantly learning from José and each year I invite him to speak in my classes to help my students expand their knowledge as well.

In José's Words

My name is José and my gender pronouns are he, him, his. I identify as a cisgender, heterosexual, male, hearing, temporarily able-bodied person, U.S. citizen, currently pursuing a doctorate degree. I am a multi-ethnic person of color. My mother was born in the U.S. and identifies as Mexican and Italian. My father was born in the Philippines; he identifies as Filipino and Indigenous. We are enrolled members of the Confederated Tribes of Siletz located in the western and southern regions of Oregon, and our ancestors are from the Galice Creek and Rogue Rivers Tribes. This form of introduction is part of locating myself within the work and space I occupy. It helps me stay aware of the power and privilege I hold. It can also signal to people that I have an awareness of how identity intersects across social and cultural domains.

I have been fortunate to be a social worker for over 18 years. During those years I have spent time working as a bilingual community mental health clinician, a field instructor, clinical supervisor, consultant, and program developer. I have also served as a full-time lecturer in an MSW department for nine years. I am honored and humbled to have worked and collaborated with a diverse range of people and communities. I feel lucky to get to do this work, to have encountered so many people who have taught me what it means to be vulnerable, resilient, and courageous; people and communities who have graciously and generously shared with me their traditions, language, food, humor, knowledge, creativity, and much more.

Naveen

I (Dana) had the good fortune of meeting Dr. Naveen Jonathan while I was serving on the Board of Directors for the California Division of the American Association for Marriage and Family Therapy. Naveen was the president-elect and president during my term. I experienced him as hard working, humble, and wholly dedicated to the field of marriage and family therapy. He worked tirelessly serving the field at the state and national level, was a professor and supervisor, as well as a practicing clinician. Early on in our professional relationship we began to talk and to share about our work and how each of our identities intersected with and informed what we were doing. Those early conversations and sharing led to a friendship that is intentional and supportive. We make a concerted effort to talk and connect (and eat) with a small group of colleagues regularly, for check-ins and support about all things personal and MFT.

I (Jessica) met Naveen while I was still a doctoral student. He was a few years ahead of me, having already graduated from the program I was in at Loma Linda University (LLU). Whenever we went to national conferences, we would have LLU student and alumni get togethers and over time, I grew to appreciate Naveen's disarming and warm presence. His authenticity, leadership, engagement in and care about the MFT field is something I respect and feel encouraged by.

In Naveen's Words

My name is Naveen Jonathan. I identify as a thirty-something, first-generation Indian American, multilingual, Christian, single, gay, cisgender male, who became an only child, born to immigrant parents from India who instilled hard work, humility, a spirit of doing for others, family relationships, and faith in God as core guiding principles, which also exist prominently in my life. My experiences with these identities have been a source of much intersectional conflict, where early on I spent much time figuring out the fit of these pieces in my life to maintain congruence with myself. Yet I still constantly find myself discerning which identities to give privilege to and which to silence, depending on the contexts, communities, individuals, and systems that I interact with. At times these identities altogether and sometimes just parts have resulted in my being discriminated against in both my personal and professional life from individuals and groups who do not know how to make sense of me as my existence somehow challenges them in many ways. At times with these identities I am seen as the expert, which when I am invited to speak on, I am glad to do so, yet other times begrudgingly do so when I am called to represent as a token member of that community. I also identify as an east coast minded democrat grounded in social justice, who grew up in the Washington, D.C. area and was transplanted 15 years ago, to a Southern California world, which has not always been understanding to my ideas. I am the first person in my family to have achieved a doctoral degree and corresponding student loan debt as well as enter into a career in the mental health field. I do come from a long line of educators and church workers in my family who combined education and faith to train individuals to serve those in need. I know my spirit and passion as an educator, supervisor, and marriage and family therapist comes from this same spirit that has been transmitted through the generations in my family system, despite my carrying it forward in the way I know is best authentic to me.

Valerie

I (Dana) met Valerie when we were both doctoral students in Virginia. We entered our program the same year and were members of an intimate cohort of five, three females and two males. Early on Valerie and I connected, but I am not sure words could help me to explain why. It was just a sense of shared values, beliefs, and commitment. I have never met anyone with a heart and intuition like Valerie. We spent many hours together talking and exploring topics such as feminism in family therapy, racial identity, relationships, statistics, and so much more. Not only her support, but her wisdom guided me through those early years in the field. I still consider her a dear friend and a sounding board.

In Valerie's Words

I am Valerie Glass. I have practiced as a therapist in a variety of social settings since 1998. I have worked in a women's health clinic, a domestic violence shelter, at an HIV+/AIDS clinic, in a mental health community services agency with children and adolescents (crisis counseling, in-home therapy, outpatient therapy), on an online platform, and through university marriage and family therapy program settings. I have been working as a professor at Northcentral University for over five years. In this position, I teach and supervise graduate students in marriage and family therapy. I currently live in the Appalachian mountains of Virginia. I identify as a sexual minority and also identify as a single parent.

DeAnna

DeAnna and I (Jessica) met while we were in the same cohort of AAMFT Minority Fellowship Program fellows. I was drawn to her for her unapologetic way of being herself in the world. I felt a connection to her over the years whenever we would see each other at conferences; I sensed there was an unspoken respect and support of one another as two doctoral students of color who had graduated, had become faculty members, and were trying to make a difference in our own contexts. Most recently, it was a privilege to serve alongside DeAnna on the AAMFT Elections Council as I was heading out and she was beginning her service. In a national leadership context, it is a gift to know that your co-leaders understand issues of diversity and equity. I feel a burst of energy and support whenever I get the chance to cross paths with her.

I (Dana) had the privilege of meeting DeAnna at a conference in recent years. We were introduced through Jessica and somehow hit it off. DeAnna is an engaging, open, and forthright person. From our first conversation, I felt both supported and challenged by her thinking and way of being. I found her to be inspiring. Our relationship has really been maintained via brief encounters at annual conferences each year, but I will say every year we deepen the conversations and the activities that we do—just recently we went the African American History museum in Washington D.C. and shared an exploration into each of our African ancestors' past.

In DeAnna's Words

My name is DeAnna Harris-McKoy. I am a cisgender, heterosexual, married, able-bodied, African American woman from a working-class background. I have practiced in a variety of settings including schools, residential treatment centers, non-profit agencies, mobile therapy, and in private practice.

Julia

Julia and I (Jessica) met while we were at a People of Color group at an American Family Therapy Academy (AFTA) conference. In these spaces, there are still few Asian/Asian American therapists and we both experienced many microaggressions. Somehow we connected and we both remember feeling such a breath of fresh air to feel understood and seen. We keep in touch through social media and check in from time to time to ask if we might be seeing each other at the next conference. There are many reasons that Asian Americans are less involved in diversity and equity work so to know that Julia is actively engaged in such work is an encouragement to me and I feel that I am not alone. For this I am so grateful.

In Julia's Words

I immigrated to the United States from Hong Kong in 1993 at the age of 17. While I had had years of classroom English prior to my arrival, my education, which was largely informed by colonialism and capitalism, had not provided me with the basic language and knowledge when it came to the racial landscape in America. I recall reading a posting in a university psychology department seeking "Caucasians" for a research study. I did not know what Caucasian meant and thought I could participate and earn a quick $50! Of course I was aware of race but my awareness was superficial and lacking in critical consciousness. I thought to be American meant to be White. All the others, like myself, were exactly that—the others, and less than. My early years here involved a lot of hard work to be more "American"—I worked on my accent relentlessly, and stopped listening to the Cantopop music that I grew up listening to. It would have been my nightmare to be perceived as "fresh off the boat." It took me years of learning to unlearn my internalized inferiority. I attribute much of my growth to my social work education, learning from peers and elders of color, and my family therapy training. I completed a postgraduate family therapy training program at the Ackerman Institute for Family, and have been teaching there since 2012.

Yajaira

Yajaira and I (Jessica) met while we were both AAMFT Minority Fellowship Program fellows. I recall that she was a returning fellow during my first year. I remember admiring her courage and the way she used her voice. We have kept in touch over the years through conferences and text messages. In one particular conference session, she was the moderator and in a dialogue setting where I felt unseen, she lifted me up and created space for my voice. This was particularly meaningful to me in my identity as an Asian American woman. I have always felt her being an encouragement and champion with and for me. It is a gift to reconnect whenever we see each other and know there is no pretense or guards to put up when we catch up.

I (Dana) was introduced to Yajaira by Jessica at an AFTA conference a few years ago, in a People of Color group meeting. I remember feeling an immediate sense of awe when Yajaira spoke. Her words and her perspective were informative, sensitive, and wise. Yajaira is someone I have connected with at conferences over the years and am now most fortunate to call a colleague, because she is teaching close by in California. Yajaira serves as a great example and support to me in the social justice teaching and work we do for the field of MFT.

In Yajaira's Words

My name is Yajaira S. Curiel and I am core faculty at the University of Southern California in the Masters of Marriage and Family Therapy program. Unfortunately, I am not clinically active at the moment due to a move to California, where I plan to transfer my Michigan LMFT. However, I have practiced, supervised and taught in the field of Couple and Family Therapy for eight years. I hold many social locations that are varied and complex. I am a first-generation Chicana, that identifies as mestiza and understands the complexity of my light-skinned complexion. I am a cisgender female who is highly educated as I have both a master's and doctoral degree in Family Therapy. I am heterosexually married, a practicing Catholic and able bodied. I am also bilingual in Spanish and English and a naturally born citizen of the USA.

Cultural Humility

The first question we asked our colleagues to respond to was: How do you remain culturally humble in your work, whether a professor, a supervisor, or a clinician (or all three)? You will see from the responses there is a lot of overlap amongst the group. Each person shared the importance of remaining open and curious to what others have to teach us about their own experiences. Another theme apparent in several responses was that of keeping the self in check—knowing that there are dominant discourses at work in each of lives and that there is always more to learn. To be culturally humble is to acknowledge the lifelong commitment to learning about ourselves and others. **José** started with the following response: For me, this is an active and ongoing process, one that begins by always acknowledging Indigenous people as the original caretakers of the land. I must recognize that the land I occupy are the traditional territories of Indigenous sovereign nations. This is an important and significant component of being humble because it serves to de-link from the settler colonial narratives which aim to eliminate Indigenous people.

José continued sharing this: I believe being culturally humble is a relational practice and personal stance of being critically conscious and accountable with regard to the ways I receive explicit and implicit material advantages from settler colonialism, imperialism, cis-heteropatriarchy, capitalism, ableism, audism, and other oppressive structures. Being culturally humble is an evolving practice that requires me to unlearn dominant narratives and binary thinking that place unfair constraints onto many people and communities. It requires me to put in constant work and effort to develop my understanding of the operations of structural power, with the aim of de-centering cis-hetero-male dominated viewpoints. It challenges me to be a reflexive and an active listener to the experiences and stories of those whose voices are most often silenced and erased. Trying to remain culturally humble requires support, honesty, and sincerity, in all of my interactions.

Naveen shared the following: I remain culturally humble, I feel by operating from my theoretical orientation. Being a solution-focused/post-modern practitioner, I am very careful to not be the expert in my client's life. I spend time noticing and listening to the client's language that they use. I pay attention to the meanings of what they say. I also invite the client to share their story. The narratives of their life carry much meaning and give me insight into experiences of oppression and lived experience. I do much of the same in other aspects of my professional life, such as working with students, colleagues, and others. I find myself naturally curious about people and what makes them who they are.

Valerie shared the following: I constantly check myself. I work to maintain an open mind with all clients and really hear their perspectives, their understanding of the world. I think this comes to play when working with MFT supervisees who are "different" than me and the client is "different" from me and the therapist. I work to embrace our differences and better understand how we see all the world. Also, I feel I celebrate uniquenesses. This is part of my personality and my upbringing. I feel—as a therapist, as a teacher, and as a supervisor—being able to really integrate the "whole" of the person into what they are doing makes a difference in their (and my) growth.

Valerie added this: I feel at times when I watch a new therapist in training, I have to step back and learn more about their perspective. It is that element of who they are that makes them a good therapist. I can't put an expectation on them to fit into a box, I have to embrace what they bring. This is essential to the therapist's developmental process (that integration of knowledge and self into their work).

DeAnna shared this: Being culturally humble is a lifelong process made up of daily conscious decisions. It was so easy for me to get lost in the larger fight for equity and justice that I did not critically analyze my everyday actions. Recently, I have been intentionally trying to align my behavior with my values which means giving up items or ideologies that oppress others.

Julia shared her ongoing development of cultural humility: I strive to remain culturally humble but recognize that moments of conceit and pride are unavoidable. When these moments arise, my mind is made up. I believe I am right and stop being curious. Relationships then get stuck. A recent struggle I had is with an Argentinian American colleague who tries very hard to connect with people of color by focusing on her marginalized identity as an immigrant, and not acknowledging her light/white-skinned privilege at all. I get so frustrated with her. I am convinced that I "know" more than her, and that I am "further along" some hypothetical racial wokeness barometer. Not only did my humility go out the window, so did my compassion. To find humility and compassion again, I need to first recognize when these moments arise, take a few mindful breaths, and recognize that I, like her, am also learning, and she, like me, is also impacted by oppression and trying to make sense of it all. I also would seek support and guidance from peers and elders as it is impossible to do this work without a community.

Yajaira's thoughts on cultural humility offer insight from the perspective of someone with both privileged and marginalized statuses. In her words: Staying culturally humble, culturally sensitive and aware of the many complexities of power, privilege, and human diversity is an ongoing process. I can honestly say that my teaching and work with students provides me a very important avenue to continue to stay engaged in this work. I constantly have to wrestle with my own intersecting identities and how I show up not only in my classroom but in all of my relationships. My desire to be a model to my students is what motivates me to challenge myself constantly, asking myself, which social location(s) are showing up right now? What power or privilege do I have in this context or interaction that I need to be sensitive to? How can I position myself in this relationship or interaction that leads from a place of humility and curiosity? My desire to not overshadow someone's pain or further re-create any trauma in someone's life is extremely important to me, so this is something I am constantly paying attention to.

Yajaira went on to share: Similarly, when I am in positions in which I hold a place of subjugation I try to stay centered in my own experience. I hope to honor the pain or hurt that I am experiencing. In those interactions my desire is that the other person involved will have enough sensitivity to engage in a process of exploration about the implications of their words or behavior in our relationship. Staying engaged in a difficult dialogue, for all parties, when there has been a relational transgression increases the trustworthiness in a relationship, even if it takes some time to reach true understanding, compassion, and resolution.

Accountability

We asked our colleagues about what helps them to remain accountable in their work to remain critically conscious. Accountability, as many of the responses highlight, requires an open mind, heart, and hands. It means that we must hold ourselves to a certain level of critical consciousness. Each person shared the importance of engaging with others who can help us when we struggle and who can support us as we navigate this journey. **José** offered his initial thoughts: This is such an important question! Similarly to being culturally humble, I believe accountability must develop into an ongoing habit consisting of critical self-reflection, seeking out meaningful honest feedback, and enacting behaviors and practices that disrupt traditional power hierarchies. While I am continuing to evolve my practice and understanding of accountability, I have incorporated those strategies into my daily routine. To add to this, I have recently been influenced by the critical work of Dr. Leigh Patel (2015) who introduced the idea of answerability. According to Patel (2015) "Answerability includes aspects of being responsible, accountable, and being part of an exchange. It is a concept that can help to maintain the coming-into-being with, being in conversation with" (p. 73).

Jose continued: Whereas my initial ideas focused on what I could do as an individual to address my power and privilege, it also seemed to ignore that I am in relationship with others and thus answerable to those relations. I appreciate Patel's view because answerability centers the importance of relationship which is essential for effective clinical practice. I am part of "an exchange" and thus have to reflect on how I am answerable to this exchange, not just my personal power. Broadening the scope, Patel (2015) asks us to "think about how our actions, our research agendas, the knowledge we contribute, can undo coloniality and create spaces for ways of being in relation that are not about individualism, ranking, and status" (p. 73). This gives me options and hope to re-think and re-imagine my "ways of being" from a decolonial perspective. I can explore decolonial shifts in my practice, that according to Eve Tuck (who wrote the introduction to Patel's book), help me to be "answerable to Indigenous people, answerable to colonized peoples on Indigenous land, and answerable to Black people on Indigenous land" (Patel, 2015, p. xv).

Naveen highlighted the importance of his relationships that help to keep him accountable: I remain accountable, in a number of ways. As mentioned above, my colleagues who do work in social justice are my biggest support system. I have had colleagues who have recommended that I try approaching an issue in a different way or the next time when faced with an issue, that I consider another option. In addition, I think of myself as a lifelong learner. I am always developing myself by attending events, reading literature, and engaging with individuals who identify differently than myself. I do this to gain more of an understanding about the lived experience of these individuals. I keep in mind individuals that identify similarly to myself. I don't want to make any assumptions about my lived experience being the same as theirs, so I keep in mind areas of similarity and also areas of difference in narratives of their lives. I also check myself when I feel uncomfortable with any issue that comes up in the classroom or therapy room, asking myself why I felt the way I did. Self-exploration and self-reflection, I feel are so key to this work.

Valerie shared some of the challenges she has with accountability and how she is able to overcome them: I think holding myself accountable is difficult at times. I find my instincts let me know if something is "off," so part of this is just being able to bring up difficult conversations with those in front of me. I think what plays a role in accountability is a willingness to listen and look for those uncomfortable moments. I feel that it is important to be able to accept that I have some work to do or changes to make. I feel cultural humility is a life-long journey.

DeAnna shared that deeply understanding intersectionality keeps her accountable. She said: As a person with multiple identities that are marginalized, I forget about some of my privileged identities. I have to continually check myself about my classist or elitist thoughts and actions. I also actively seek opportunities and environments that challenge my way of thinking.

Julia offered a response with suggestions that are helpful to all of us. She said: To remain accountable, I try to be aware of my power and privilege that come with being a therapist, teacher/supervisor, U.S. citizen, cisgender, heterosexual, light-skinned, multilingual, middle-class, and overall healthy. I, like many others who are committed to anti-oppression work, aspire to not misuse my power and be culturally sensitive. However, such aspirations are easier said than done. Amongst the many concepts that I have learned from Kenneth V. Hardy, I found these three concepts to be particularly helpful in my effort to remain accountable. In any context talk, i.e., dialogue that involves dimension of diversity: (1) Name and claim the particular issue or dimension of oppression, such as race or class. (2) Most of us have a tendency to default to our subjugated selves. (3) While both parties bear responsibility to the context talk, the one who bears more power of the particular dimension of oppression being discussed also bears more responsibility. Often, my subjugated identities, the hurt and triggers that are associated with them, preclude me from owning the power that comes with my privileged identities. These three concepts, along with feedback from my elders, peers, clients, and trainees, help me remain accountable.

Support Systems

For the last question, we asked our colleagues about their support systems. Every single one responded with an emphasis about how important support is for their success, both personally and professionally. You will also notice that there is an emphasis on self-care as well. **José** offered a beautifully thoughtful and well-rounded response: It has taken some time for me to realize that my support system really begins with me and the choices I make to take care of myself. A good reminder of this was listening to Erykah Badu during an interview on the podcast What's Good with Stretch & Bobbito (Armstrong & Garcia, 2018) where she described her daily self-care support system. She said,

> I make sure that I get the five doctors in every day—a little sun, Dr. Sun ... Dr. Nutrition make sure I'm eating right and drinking a lot of water. Dr. Exercise, you know, in the morning getting the gym in or the yoga, whatever it is or walking or whatever. Spirit part, where I'm alone in my car, and I am able to communicate ... With the higher things. And then, five, just Dr. Breath,

making sure I'm breathing correctly. So I try to get all of that in every day.

José said: I found this to be a useful way to think about support systems because it embraces our relationship with nature, food, and "higher things," and it is something that needs to put into action on the daily.

José continued with the following: Thinking of myself in relation to my support system fills me with joy and love. I am truly blessed to have these people and community in my life. My support system includes my wife, family, pets, friends, and colleagues. Their love, kindness, nurturing, and honest feedback have been critical pillars of support throughout my life. I also count on support from my relatives and ancestors who are no longer here, but whose stories and experiences live on through storytelling, photos, and videos. I call on them regularly. I include nature and art as critical to my support system. It could be a landscape, mountains, the ocean, clouds, trees, or plants; it could be music, film, television, paintings, poems, books, sculpture, architecture, etc. All of these have provided me with options, alternatives, counternarratives, and spaces for inspiration. Lastly, I would include the stories of courage and determination from the people and communities I've never met, but nonetheless whose leadership and sacrifice in the face of insurmountable odds fills me with admiration and hope.

Naveen shared about the importance of his relationships with colleagues: My biggest support system, are a few colleagues who do work in therapy and in classroom instruction around social justice. These colleagues are ones that I reach out to consult on cases, to seek additional resources whether for therapy or in my classroom. With these colleagues, I can also discuss various issues that take place in society as often these issues impact clients, students, faculty, and those around us.

Valerie agreed with Naveen stating: My biggest support system when it comes to cultural humility is typically my colleagues. Being able to bring up sensitive topics or difficult ideas that play a role on my work and share my perspectives helps me to grow and become more humble.

DeAnna humbly stated: My support system consists of my husband, family, friends, colleagues, mentors, and mentees. I am constantly amazed by the people in my life and grateful that they actively choose to be in my circle.

Julia delineated her response between professional support and personal support sharing about professional first: My professional support system consists of peers and elders of color and some White allies at the

Ackerman Institute, and other colleagues whom I have met over the years through the Eikenberg Academy for Social Justice. As an Asian woman with most of my academic and professional experiences in White settings, I was used to feeling invisible, stereotyped, and not valued. It was in social and racial justice spaces where I began to have a different experience, and my voice is welcomed rather than being perceived as disrespectful. As Asians are often underrepresented in mixed race social justice spaces, my mentors and peers have been mostly African American and Latinx of different races. It was not until recently when I had the opportunity to connect with other Asian Americans who are committed to social justice. The experience to be with my people in this context has been powerful and healing.

Julia went on to share about her personal support system: My personal support consists of my White partner who has struggled with me over the years. Our conversations on race have been challenging, and I appreciate that fact that we keep on having them. I think both of us have learned and grown from our interracial partnership. Our 5-year-old Biracial son is also part of my support system. Being in his presence and seeing the world through his eyes gives me strength and hope on days when I need them most. Other personal support includes Buddhist teachings, close friends near and afar, a long-term therapist, and other parents who are also committed to raising justice conscious children.

Yajaira's response highlights how accountability and support systems go hand-in-hand. She shared the following insight: Overall, I rely on my friends and colleagues with whom I have done much of my family therapy training. I trust them in their own pursuits to be social justice advocates and I know that they will easily call me on my own blind spots or help me create space to engage in difficult dialogues when necessary. Since we are all committed to the important work of being social justice advocates, we work diligently separately, in our own spaces and places, bringing attention to injustice, trauma, and voicelessness. I also try to engage in important events like trainings and conferences that continue to discuss important topics related to social justice. In these times, my goal is to attend workshops that challenge me to struggle with areas of privilege in my life and also help me rejuvenate and restore the places in which I have experienced pain and trauma. None of this would be possible if I had not done the previous self-work of critically interrogating and understanding my intersecting identities and their respective areas of privilege and/or subjugation.

Summary

The voices from our colleagues in the field represent but a small portion of those who are dedicated to the raising of critical consciousness, maintaining cultural humility, and who are socially just in their work with colleagues, students, supervisees, and clients. Each one stressed that relationships are paramount to their commitment and longevity in the field. They, like us, turn to others for support and accountability, for authentic and meaningful connections, for their own growth, and to enable them to continue to facilitate the growth of others. Each one of them reiterated that their learning requires intentionality and creating *space*—it is lifelong, centered in genuine curiosity, embracing differences, celebrating uniqueness, remaining and holding others accountable, and owning and regularly checking their personal power and privilege. The key factor in all of this is the relational piece—the reflexive relationship with the *self*, and the transformative relationships with others.

Wrap-Up

First, we want to acknowledge how far you've come as a reader of this book. We hope you feel supported, challenged, encouraged, and motivated as you continue forward on your journey. Our ultimate goal at the beginning and end is that you have found ways to deepen your understanding of your whole self as a person and as a therapist and that you have been inspired to make purposeful connections with others who can walk beside you on your career journey. We understand the feeling of being a tiny new part of this large field. Should you see or know that we are at any of the national conferences, please don't hesitate to introduce yourself to us. Have courage to reach out to those whose stories resonated with you. Seek connection in the unexpected places! You probably chose the MFT field, knowing that you would have the honor of walking alongside people in their deepest pain and grief as well as celebrating their growth and healing. Our hope for each of us is that in our desire to witness healing and transformation in others, it begins first in us. We wish for you an MFT journey where sooner than later, you can access your whole beautiful, sociocontextual self so that your voice and presence shines fully with your peers, colleagues, mentors, supervisors, and most importantly your clients.

References

Armstrong, S., & Garcia, B. (Hosts). (2018, August 15). What's Good with Stretch & Bobbito: Erykah Badu. [Audio podcast]. Retrieved from www.npr.org/podcasts/510323/whats-good-with-stretch-and-bobbito

Patel, L. (2015). *Decolonizing educational research: From ownership to answerability*. New York: Routledge.

Wilkins, E. J., Whiting, J. B., Watson, M. F., Russon, J. M., & Moncrief, A. M. (2013). Residual effects of slavery: What clincians need to know. *Contemporary Family Therapy*, 35(1), 14–28.

Appendix: List of Resources

This is a beginning-level list of resources to direct you to supportive professional organizations and book readings.

Professional Organizations

American Family Therapy Academy (AFTA)	www.afta.org
American Association for Marriage and Family Therapists (AAMFT)	www.aamft.org
APA Society for the Psychological Study of Culture, Ethnicity, and Race	http://division45.org
Asian American Psychological Association	www.aapaonline.org
International Family Therapy Association	www.ifta-familytherapy.org/
The Association of Black Psychologists	www.abpsi.org

Appendix 173

Recommended Book Readings

Title	Author(s)
A People's History of the United States	Howard Zinn
Birth of a White Nation: The Invention of White People and its Relevance Today	Jacqueline Battalora
Culturally Sensitive Supervision and Training: Diverse Perspectives and Practical Applications	Edited by Kenneth Hardy & Toby Bobes
An Indigenous People's History of the United States	Roxanne Dunbar-Ortiz
Liberation Based Healing Practices	Rhea Almeida
Readings for Diversity and Social Justice (4th ed.)	Edited by Maurianne Adams, Warren J. Blumenfeld, D. Chase J. Catalano, Keri Dejong, Heather W. Hackman, Larissa E. Hopkins, Barbara Love, Madeline L. Peters, Davey Shlasko, & Ximena Zuniga (Editor)
Socioculturally Attuned Family Therapy: Guidelines for Equitable Theory and Practice	Teresa McDowell, Carmen Knudson-Martin, & J. Maria Bermudez
Transformative Family Therapy: Just Families in a Just Society	Rhea Almeida, Ken Dolan-Del Vecchio, & Lynn Parker
Voices of Color: First-Person Accounts of Ethnic Minority Therapists	Edited by Mudita Rastogi & Elizabeth Wieling
"Why are all the Black kids sitting together in the cafeteria?": And other conversations about race	Beverly Daniel Tatum

Index

Locators in *italic* refer to figures, locators in **bold** refer to tables.

accountability 39, 47, 149, 155, 165–166, 169, 170
ADDRESSING framework 79, 108–110
African Americans 79, *117*, 160, 169
Aponte, Harry 3, 17
Armenians 82, 83–84
Asian Americans 9, 22–25, 32, 35, 40, 56, 91–92, 140, 149, *152–153*, 160–161
attunement 145, 147
authenticity 6–7, 71, 82, 158

bias *see* implicit bias
biracial 25, 27, 30, 36–37, 39–40, 56, 107, 169
Bowen, Murray 20, 115, 139
Brown, Brené 7

call-out culture 102
Catholics 89, 162
Christians 21–22, 30, 33–34, 41, *124*, 158
cisgender 21, 25, 79, 82, 89, 91, 93, 100–102, 114, 157–158, 160, 162, 167
cisheteropatriarchy 22, 99, 114, 140, 163
civility 39, 141–142, 145, 146
classroom 32, 55, 61, 63, 65–66, 89, 101, 128

clinical courage 33, 141
COAMFTE 39, 48–49, 61–63, 79
Colonial Mentality Scale (CMS) 111
colonialism 8, 111, 156
colonization 21, 111, 123
Commission on Accreditation for Marriage and Family Therapy Education *see* COAMFTE
contextual consciousness 9
contextual differentiation 9–10, 25, 31, 32, 37, 88, 139–140
Crenshaw, Kimberlé 12, 17
CritG *see* genograms, critical genograms
critical consciousness 9–10, 22, 24–25, 30, 35, 40, 47, 53–54, 73, 82, 91, 93, 96, 104–106, 108, 120–121, 123, 133–134, 136–137, 144, 151, 161, 170
Critical Mixed Race 38
cultural bumps 66
cultural humility 10, 162, 164, 166, 168
cultural genograms *see* genograms
culture 10–11, 16, 20, 22, 31, 33, 36, 43–44, 47–48, 53, 60, 63, 72–73, 82–84, 87, 96, 102, 107, 109, 111–112, 115–**119**, 128, 129, 130–131, 140
curriculum 62, 74

discourses 6, 16, 35–37, 89, 99, 106, 107, 133; dominant 11–12, 37, 89, 99, 104–105, 148, 162
discrimination 47, 54, 93, 108, 122
diversity 11, 13, 28, 40, 60–62, 66, 78, 94–95, 125, 142–143, 160, 164, 167, 174; cultural 44–45; courses 48, 62–64, 101–102; in supervision 71–73; training 35, 48, 52–54
dysconsciousness 41

empowerment 3, 15, 60, 77, 92–93
equifinality 5
equity 5–6, 11, 15, 40, 47–48, 61–62, 114, 142–143, 160–161, 164
Ethiopians 87–88
ethnic minority 32, 45, 52–57, 106, 173
ethnicity 12, 16, 53, 116, 125, 172; courses 61–65; supervision 69, 72
evangelical/evangelicalism 22, 33, 45

family system 4–5, **119**, 159; *see also* Bowen, Murray
feminism 28, 114–115, 159
feminist *see* feminism
feminist informed supervision *see* supervision
Filipinos 56, 111–112, 157
Freire, Paolo 10

gender expression 113–114
gender identity 34, 61, 101–104, 107, 109, 113–114
genderqueer 100, 113
generation 16, 65, 109; first-generation college student 25–26, 37,96, 97, 99; first-generation immigrant 83, 87, *124*, 158,162; second-generation immigrant 21, 82–84, 91, 93
genograms 115; critical genograms 120–*124*; cultural genograms 116–**119**

Hardy, Kenneth 11, 15, 16, 64, 112, 116–118, 125, 167, 173
heteronormativity 89, 129
heteropatriarchy *see* cisheteropatriarchy
heterosexism 13, 129
high-context cultures 130–131
historical trauma *see* trauma
homophobia 33, 129

immersion experiences 63, 66
Implicit Association Test 127
implicit bias 13, 46, 51, 57, 92, 127, 130, 133–134
inclusion 11, 47, 48, 61, 102
Indian Americans 158
Indigenous identity 9, 107–111, 147, 156–157, 162–163, 166, 173
international student 44–45, 84, 128
intersectionality 12, 17, 46, 52, 65, 79, 80, 137, 166
Iranians 93–95
Islamophobia 93
Italians 157

journaling 2, 65–66, 121

Knudson-Martin, Carmen 5, 9, 14, 31, 63, 65, 173
Koreans 31, 91

Low-and High-Context Communication Scale 131–132,
low-context cultures 130–131

marginalization 15–16, 21, 35–36, 47, 55, 61, 65, 73, 102–104, 135, 140, 154; identity 2, 43, 45, 57, 77, 104, 148, 164
McDowell, Teresa 9, 11, 13, 14, 52–55, 62–63, 65–67, 73, 173
McIntosh, Peggy 14
mentorship 37, 48, 52–53, 67, 74, 158; lack of 53
Mexicans 55, 96–97, 99, *117*, 157
microaggressions 30, 36, 45, 77–78, 160
Muslims 93–96, 127, 147

Narrative Therapy 140

openness 2, 16, 24, 33, 50, 80, 142
oppression 46, 65, 72, 106–108, 112, 118, 122, 163–164, 167; systemic 13–15, 111, 120, 129

patriarchy 113–114
person/people of color 34, 35–37, 64, 87–88, 157, 160, 162, 164; student of color 20, 81, 108, 160; therapist of color 35, 56, 67, 106
personal sociocultural awareness 141, 144–146

power 10, 12–14, 15, 24, 29, 63, 65, 102, 114, 120–121, 164–167; gender and 31, 33, *124*; relational 5–6, 14, 57, 82, 138, 145, 147–148, 157; supervision 44, 51–52, 70–73
privilege 14, 25, 34, 35, 46, 65, 102, 108, 115, 120–121, 133–134; white privilege 22, 27, 62, 126

queer identity 12, 33, 45–46, 89–91, 100, 102, 129

race 12, 14–15, 22, 27, 33, 37, 54, 64, 112; in supervision 73; *see also* genograms
racial identity 109, 112–113
racism 13, 27, 53, 55–57, 64–65, 67, 73, 93, 120, 122, 126–127; internalized 56, 145
racist 12, 30, 45, 53, 126
relational sociocultural curiosity 143
Relational Support Diagram 152–*153*

Satir, Virginia 3–4
self-awareness 3, 32, 64–66
self-of-the-therapist 3–4, 68, 71, 82, 107, 138
self-reflection 2, 46, 63, 64, 74, 121, 144, 165–166
SERT *see* Socio-Cultural Relationship Therapy
settler colonialism *see* colonialism
sexism *see* patriarchy
sexual identity 107, 129–130
sexual orientation 34, 53, 89–90, 109, 118, 129–130
social context 5–6, 8, 9, 25, 106, 121–123

social justice 15, 40, 44, 72, 103–104, 113, 158, 162, 166, 168–169
social location 5, 10, 13, 15–16, 23, 27, 35–37, 43, 49, 52–53, 57, 73–75, 78–79, 90, 92–93, 105–107, 120–123, 130, 142–144, 148, 162, 164
sociocultural interest 142–143, 145–147
socioeconomic status 9, 16, 55, 61, 63, 82, 107, 108, 109, *124*
Socio-Emotional Relationship Therapy 5
Stages of Sociocultural Relational Connection 141, **145**–146, 149
student(s) of color *see* person/people of color
supervision 48, 36, 68–71, 75; feminist informed 72; individual 51; multicultural 72, 73, 173
supervision experience 23–24, 48, 52, 79, 84, 90, 97, 98, 100; meaningful/best 49–50, 69, 70; challenging/worst 42, 49, 52–57
supervisory relationship *see* supervision
support system 58, 151–152, 166–169
systemic oppression *see* oppression
systems theory 4, 107

Taiwanese 21–22, 84
training experiences *see* supervision experience
trans/transgender identity 77, 100–104, 114, 134
trauma 42, 47, 87, 109, 148, 165, 169

vulnerability 7, 80, 148

White, Michael 28, 141